HOW TO
RECRUIT GOOD
MANAGERS

HOW TO RECRUIT GOOD MANAGERS

And How To Keep Them

ROBERT S REDMOND

KOGAN
PAGE

First published in Great Britain in 1989 by Kogan Page Limited, 120 Pentonville
Road, London N1 9JN.

British Library Cataloguing in Publication Data

Redmond, Robert S.
  How to recruit good managers – and how
  to keep them
  1. Great Britain. Industries. Managers.
  Recruitment & selection
  I. Title
  658.4'0711'0941

  ISBN 1–85091–903–8
  ISBN 1–85091–904–6 Pbk

Printed and bound in Great Britain by
Biddles Limited, Guildford

Contents

INTRODUCTION

This book is not written for the use of the experienced personnel officer of the big company. It is intended to help the proprietor or chief executive of the small- to medium-sized firm (and even the line manager of the big one) who is faced with:

- a need to recruit into management for the first time
- a management problem caused by growth of the firm
- a deficiency in one or more of the team.

It begins from a consideration of the factors which should be taken into account before any recruitment plan is drawn up; whether, in fact, there really is a vacancy and who and what is wanted.

A reading of recruitment advertising in the press always reveals a number of firms who announce management vacancies and yet do not seem to be sure exactly what kind of experience and qualifications they seek. Some actual examples are given in support of this argument. If only the top management of these companies had spent a little more time in thought before buying expensive space in the media, they might have run less risk of disappointment with the result.

Recruitment and selection are two parts of the process of finding the right people. First, candidates for a job are *recruited* and then a *selection* is made from among them. The several steps to be taken in each part are described.

There is no magic wand available to the employer. No one can ever guarantee success in recruitment and selection. The consultant or the agency, for instance, who says it can be done must be either a charlatan or a fool. At the same time, the odds against finding a square peg for a square hole can be shortened if some commonsense rules are followed. These are set out in the early chapters.

Care in the early stages of recruitment and, in particular, in preparation of the job specification will help in attracting applicants of the right quality rather than in large numbers. This makes selection much less time-consuming and yet more likely to succeed.

There are always risks in trying to cut corners and time needs to be spent in preparing for interviews. At this stage and in the interview itself, that job specification is an essential tool.

Finally, in the recruitment process, suggestions are offered for avoidance of that exasperating procrastination by some candidates when they are offered a job.

Having appointed good people, the best firms will want to keep them. Some suggestions for this are offered.

The competent personnel manager has a knowledge of the pitfalls of the laws about discrimination (race and sex) and others in the field of employee relations. The big company, therefore, ought never to be caught out. Yet the law applies with equal force to the small firm where there is no in-house expertise. It is hoped that this book will be of help in showing some of the traps awaiting the unwary and, in the appendices, some sources of advice are offered. There is no pretence that it is a textbook on employment law. It merely tries to point the reader in the right direction and to preserve inter-personal relationships in a company.

It is sad to read reports of the failure of some businesses attributed to shortage of capital. One wonders how often the real reason has been a lack of competent management control of the assets. Could these firms not have been saved if they had new or better trained managers at the right level and at the right time? Could some of them have avoided difficulty by recognising danger signals and instituting a management development programme in the early stages of trouble?

There is no real agreement on a definition of the 'small firm'. Is it related to turnover, capital, numbers employed, or what? A definition which suits one set of circumstances or organisation – even a political argument – may not be acceptable to another. So far as this book is concerned, a small firm is one where there is no personnel department and where the proprietor, partners or board of directors – even departmental line managers – have to cover that function in addition to looking after their main and principal functions.

It might be wise to explain what is meant by the word 'manager'. A definition given in the *Concise Oxford English Dictionary* is: 'person conducting a business, institution etc'. Sometimes, a manager is thought to be one who supervises others. Quite often, however, the manager will have no one reporting to him or her at all. This is especially true in the small concern, and for the purpose of this book a manager is assumed to be one who is part of the decision-making process (however little initiative may be required) as opposed to the operative who always carries out instructions.

Every attempt has been made to avoid jargon. There is no use of some of those 'in' words beloved of some in big business. It is believed that the reader would prefer to be asked, 'When can you deliver the goods?' rather than, 'What are your time horizons?' Quite apart from other considerations, these 'buzz' words tend to go out of fashion. To use them would be to date the book before its time.

Nor is there any suggestion in favour of the use of so-called sophisticated techniques in interviewing or selection. Such things as aptitude tests, psychological examinations, selection boards or panels on the lines of the armed services may have their place. They are valuable when, say, a number of new graduates are being taken in from the universities to a multinational corporation. They are quite out of place when just one job is to be filled in a small- or medium-sized company.

It is hoped that what follows is a statement of common sense and little more. It is all based upon solid experience – some of it painful – in smaller companies or as a result of working as a consultant and seeing the problems and experiences of others. All the anecdotes, believe it or not, are true.

1
WHY IS THERE A VACANCY?

When a vacancy occurs in a management team, it is good sense to establish, without any self-deception, why. Whose fault is it? Time and effort spent making an honest appraisal, free from prejudice, will never be wasted. It can help to avoid further expense and the disturbance of yet another recruitment in the future.

Someone has left to develop a career

If so, do you want it to happen again? Maybe you like the idea of giving young, ambitious men and women experience – or letting them gain it at your expense. Perhaps you think this is a good way of ensuring a constant supply of fresh ideas. Big firms seldom object to young folk joining them for a few years and then moving on. They do, however, hope that they can retain the best. Small and medium-sized firms are more likely to take an opposite view. In any case, there is less scope for recruiting large numbers of school-leavers and graduates as management trainees. This leads, usually, to a preference towards finding the one whose ambition will be to grow and develop with the firm. It is wise to form a view on this point in the light of the reason for the vacancy.

You would not – or could not – delegate authority

The manager appointed to accept responsibility for the running of part (however small) of a business, who finds that every attempt at initiative is stifled, is likely to do one of two things: seek job satisfaction elsewhere or become a zombie.

Maybe it suits you and your way of doing things to keep your hands on the reins. This is fine so long as you recognise it and understand the implications. It can prevent the firm from growing since it will become impossible for you to take every single management decision. If this is what you want, it will make sense to seek the 'plodder' who will follow your instructions without question, but do little more. Do not then expect much originality of thought or action and do not expect important decisions to be taken in your absence. If this is your way of working and you appoint a 'self-starter', you may have another vacancy quite soon.

One of the most difficult situations can arise when there is a clash of ideas. Perhaps a young member of the team has what he or she thinks is a brain-wave, but you cannot go along with it. Unless your reasons are understood, there may be a lack of job satisfaction and you are at risk of being called a fuddy duddy or something worse. But it is your responsibility to make the big policy decisions and you have every right to run things as you wish. This, however, is not to say you should stifle all suggestions. They should be welcomed and reasons for rejection explained.

Someone unsuitable has gone – or been removed

Irrespective of whether an unsuitable person has been given the sack or gone of his or her own accord, it is clear that the appointment was a mistake in the first place. How did it happen? Did you, for instance, select a mechanical engineer when you should have insisted on an electrical background? Perhaps you engaged someone whose personality was wrong. The importance of compatibility can hardly be over stressed in the environment of the smaller organisation – even the small department of a big company. It is always wise to try to discover how it was that a job was given to a face that would not fit.

Someone is retiring

Succession will, of course, be planned with care and well in advance of the actual retirement date, but here is a golden opportunity for a detailed reappraisal of the whole management structure. It will almost certainly follow a long period of service. It will be by no means sure that a 'carbon copy' of the outgoing manager is what is required. This is the time to ask what needs to be done, who in the firm is available to do it, and then to seek the necessary qualifications and experience to fill the gap. If, by training and promotion, it is possible to avoid recruitment altogether, so much the better. It may, at least, be possible to see the vacancy as being lower down the line.

The vacancy is a new one

Here lies the greatest danger of an unsatisfactory solution of the problem. Someone in the existing team is going to have to delegate some responsibility. New authority can never be created, it can only be given away. Will that person – perhaps a group of people – be able and willing to do this? It is worth questioning whether there really should be an addition to the management team at this stage of the firm's development. It is not easy for the lonely entre-preneur to sit down calmly and think out every aspect of what is, after all, a human situation when there is, in any case, an overload and there are not nearly enough hours in the day. Success, however, comes to the boss who makes more right decisions than wrong ones and hasty conclusions can be dangerous.

Whether to expand a management team and how to do it depend on one's ambition. Is the firm to be allowed and encouraged to grow or should it stay small? Maybe there is no choice. It can be nice to remain as you are and a great many succeed in doing just that, to the entire satisfaction of all concerned. In other cases, the market may be demanding greater service or shorter delivery times. Failure to give customer satisfaction because a firm cannot cope can lead only to contraction or even oblivion. If expansion is the only (or desired) option then the time must come when new strength will be vital, but it is worth remembering that more businesses have failed because of over-staffing than otherwise.

The lonely proprietor of a small firm, faced with this kind of dilemma, might be advised to adopt the 'temporary' solution suggested in Chapter 9 (see page 74).

Conclusion

Vacancies in management occur for innumerable reasons. This chapter has put forward no more than suggestions. If, in all honesty, you can be absolutely sure about what has happened and why, you can go a long way towards avoiding another mistake. Recruitment and selection are expensive in both time and money and are something to be done as seldom as possible.

2
KNOW WHAT YOU WANT

'There are no decent works managers around any more.' This was said by the managing director of a small engineering company after he had hired and fired six people in as many years.

By this time, although he failed to recognise the signals, he had acquired such a reputation that no one with any self-respect would apply to his firm for any management job at all and the staff *in situ* were not very happy either.

The root of his dilemma was soon discovered by a management consultant. He was the supreme example of the entrepreneur who had founded what was really a successful business, but he had never 'thought through' the process of recruitment and selection of people to whom he could delegate authority with confidence. Nor had he ever sat down to prepare a proper job specification before he advertised a vacancy. It was a clear case of not knowing what he wanted and not being satisfied until he got it.

When it was recommended that he should see a consultant, his reaction was, 'How does *he* know better than I do what I want?' In the event, the consultant who came to see him was a woman. She explained that no one could ever guarantee success in recruitment, but the risks of failure will always be reduced if there is a clear picture of every aspect of the vacancy. The questions she asked were searching and made him think that he could have done the job himself much better if he had given more thought to this initial stage of the exercise.

The need for a job specification

Every job specification or description ought to consist of seven parts:

12

- a description of the firm
- a description of the job and how the vacancy arises
- the responsibilities to be accepted
- the authority which will be delegated to the person appointed
- the knowledge and experience required

  (a) essential
  (b) desirable

- conditions, salary and other benefits
- the prospects the firm can offer to the person in this job.

Some people will be saying all this is bureaucratic tommy rot. They do not have the time for all this palaver. They have a business to run etc. Ask yourself. Would you put an order into your works for manufacture without proper drawings or specification as to quantities and qualities?

No one suggests that you can produce a human being by moulding or extrusion to an exact pattern like a piece of metal or plastic. It can, indeed, happen that a candidate in interview will prompt a thought and thus lead to an amendment of that job description you have drafted with care. But this will happen only when the most careful thought has been given to the preparation in the first place. It is usually the good candidate's questions about some particular aspect which sparks off a new idea. This, surely, emphasises rather than diminishes the case for proper preparation.

When we come to consider interviewing candidates (Chapter 7) we shall see the value of the job specification in preventing trouble with the discrimination laws, but the main reason why our hirer and firer thought there were no decent works managers any more was that they all seemed to say, 'You never said I was expected to do that.' Given the whole thing in writing as a 'brief', no one can sustain that argument. Nor can you be accused of offering prospects or not fulfilling a promise. The evidence is there in black and white.

Look now at the example on pages 21-26. There is nothing fictional about it except the name of the company and its location. Follow the reasoning behind each section.

What is the firm?

Never be dishonest. Tell the whole truth. If you have been having a rough time, say so, but explain plans for the future and say how the vacancy arises as part of them. Lack frankness and a good candidate will soon uncover the truth or, worse, a coloured version of it. Show clearly:

- what the firm is and what it does
- how it started and when
- where it is going
- the prospects it offers to anyone joining it now.

The job

Job titles can mean almost anything. Even if a term is clear to you, it may not be so to an outsider. 'Works superintendent' in certain parts of Lancashire used to mean 'janitor'. An American company wondered why their intentions were so misunderstood when they were planning a new factory. Somehow, the right people did not seem to be applying for quite senior jobs.

The authority

Management suggests authority but, as has been said earlier, it can never be created. It can only be given away or, in other words, delegated. The one who is drafting a job specification should always ponder this point. The specimen specification sets out what one works manager was empowered to do and it defines the limits regarding:

- people
- things
- money.

Never leave anything to chance. Never decide to 'see how we get on'. Be restrictive at first if you wish. You may intend to allow authority to develop. Then say so. Every manager must know what his powers are from day 1. In writing this section, you are forced to decide whether you want a manager of vision and initiative or whether, to be honest with yourself, you would be happier with a plodder. Search your soul. Can you really delegate? If you cannot, the man or woman of initiative will not be with you for very long.

There were once two partners in a business using a raw material with a habit of rising and falling in price without much warning. Buy at the nadir and make a profit; run out of stock at the peak and make a loss.

During the absence of one partner, the other was taken ill just as the price touched bottom. When they were both back at work, it had peaked again. They blamed their accountant who had been with them for a year. They said he ought to have used his initiative. He said he had never been given the authority. The fault lay with the partners who had never thought of a situation like this when they made the appointment. In fact, the job specification, such as it was, really showed they had wanted a good bookkeeper who would control the cash flow. That is what they had got.

Responsibilities and duties

Here are two headings it may be difficult to separate. Every manager, however, needs to know:

- to whom he is responsible
- who is responsible to him.

The rest should follow naturally, but look again at the example on pages 21-26. It was drafted in the light of experience and it leaves no room for argument as to what the works manager was expected to do. The duties attached to a job should always be defined so that there is no room for misunderstanding.

Knowledge and experience

You now know what the new manager's job is and you have defined the limits. This enables you to set out the qualifications you need to attract. Once again, however, you have to realise that you are not going to mould or extrude raw material. You have got to decide what is:

(a) essential
(b) desirable

Without (a), the job cannot be done. The more of (b) the better.

Suppose that, on your shop floor, there are representatives of the ethnic communities to whom English, at best, is a second tongue. Maybe you think fluency in, say, Gujerati could be of value. But to make this an essential requirement would be too restrictive. Perhaps you would like a chartered engineer, but would HND be adequate? Be sure of the minimum and never be over-demanding. Can you afford to rule out the person with experience whose formal qualifications are on the low side?

Education

Here again, set down the minimum general education level you are prepared to accept, but recognise that the older the man or woman may be, the less O and A levels will matter.

There are many good people in management who have no formal technical education at all. They have qualified the hard way, by experience. They tend, however, to be of the older generation. To some that statement will be heresy; to others common sense. There are strong prejudices and opinions about this. Graduates of Oxbridge may think it vital that all members of management team should have the same background. Others say, 'Never mind the qualifications, can he do the job?'

You are the one who is seeking the new manager. You are the one who must decide whom you want. All that can be said is that to ask for too much can mean failure in recruitment but, nevertheless, you do want someone in whom you will have confidence.

Compatibility

Harmony and team spirit in a firm – especially a smaller one - is vital. We have already thought about your own prejudices in the field of education, but are there any others in the company whom you value and whom you know find it difficult to work with some quirks of human nature? No one suggests that others should join in your selection. That is your responsibility, but you do want someone in whom you will have confidence and whose personality will not clash with others.

External activities

More than one appointment has failed because of an outside commitment. Maybe you think that what an employee does in his or her own time is none of your business but, if you would really like someone who will enhance the local standing of your firm by doing something in a voluntary organisation, at least bear it in mind. Would you be happy with a manager who takes an active role in the affairs of a political party? If your sales manager will have a better chance of success if he has a low golf handicap, say so. This, indeed, could be listed as a 'desirable' qualification in the job specification.

Age

Never advertise for, in effect: 'not over 25, but with at least 15 years' experience.' So many seem to do so.

Start from the level of experience you must have. That will, surely, settle the lower age limit.

Now, what reasons do you have for any top limit at all? Be honest. There are only three things to consider:

- the cost of the pension scheme
- compatibility
- management succession.

In a small firm, forget the pension scheme problem. Any good insurance broker will guide you round that one.

You may be seeking someone who will grow with the company and be ready to take over a first-line responsibility in about 10 years' time. If so, there is no sense in recruiting someone over 50.

Compatibility, in this sense, suggests that you must think whether you would like to employ a man or woman old enough to be your parent. Equally, will a 55-year-old take orders happily from someone 25 years younger?

Subject to these considerations, is there any real point in

specifying an upper age limit at all?

About 10 years ago, a client told a consultant that the upper age limit for a job was 47. The reason for this was never very clear but, fortunately for the client, the consultant ignored the instruction and shortlisted a man of 57. Eight years later when this man retired at 65, he had transformed the whole organisation. Left on his own, the client might never have even considered the application.

Mobility

Sales managers, of course, will have to be away frequently in order to visit customers and to see the reps on their territories, but what about the production manager? Might he not have to dash off at short notice? If so, make it clear from the start. Confidence can be shattered if family or other problems arise at a time of crisis. The full story given to every applicant can be a safeguard, too, against the kind of difficulties outlined in Chapter 14 (on discrimination).

Conditions of service

Put yourself in the shoes of a good applicant. Would you think of asking questions about conditions when you wanted a good job? Would you not be afraid of implying a wrong attitude? ('That fellow was more interested in holiday entitlement and sickness pay . . .') Set it all out on paper and avoid any embarrassment:

- period of notice
- service agreement
- holiday entitlement
- sickness leave, private health scheme
- normal hours of work.

If you intend to allow six weeks' holiday each year, but insist on no more than a fortnight at a time, put it on paper. You have no intention of offering a service agreement? Then leave it out, but be definite in answer to any questions. Never hint and then fail to implement. An unexpected offer in the light of good service can be appreciated. Failure after a hint to become concrete can unsettle.

The cost

There is an old saying that if you pay peanuts you will get monkeys. More than one business has failed because of parsimony. You need value for money, but this does not mean salary only. You may not wish to write the full cost into the job specification, but you need to know it in order to decide the things which must go in.

Several professional firms have found that management consultants must generate fees of at least four times their annual salaries in order to break even. This, of course, includes the overheads to be carried in their profit centres. You will know these in your firm – or you should. The points for thought are items such as the following:

- salary
- commission, bonus, profit share etc
- National Insurance
- out-of-pocket expenses, travel etc.
- car or car allowance
- private health insurance
- office or other accommodation.

When you have a total for all that, you can proceed. Your aim is to find someone who will contribute to your profits by increasing efficiency or raising turnover (see Chapter 10, Spending for Profit). If the total frightens you, perhaps you have to think again and go back to the beginning:

- Should the vacancy exist at all?
- Could other job specifications be changed to fill the need?
- Could you recruit at a lower level of experience and qualification?

In fixing salary, it used to be the case that there was a 'going rate'. This is no longer so except in certain professional disciplines. Somehow, you have just got to offer the right figure for what you want in the area where the job and the firm happen to be. It may pay you to seek advice on this point from the agencies, and it is always a good idea to look at advertisements in the regional press to see what others are offering.

Status

Some people rate status very highly. I remember hearing about an assignment to recruit a company secretary. The vacancy had arisen because the directors, out of regard for a man who had given good service over two decades, decided to provide him with a company car in place of the old banger he owned. The announcement gave pleasure until the make and model in mind were revealed. If that was all he was worth, he said, he would resign. He did and got a new job with a car to match his personal assessment of status.

The moral of this story is that before any fringe benefits are offered, think. In the case quoted, the initial depreciation cost of the car would have been about £2000. A salary increase or bonus of that order would have been happily accepted and appreciated.

Prospects

Of course, everyone wants to see prospects in a job, but never say, 'It's up to you.' It seldom is – entirely. A good manager will always exploit the personal opportunities, but this can only be done within the limits offered by the firm. Your ambitions for your company have already been set out under, 'What is the firm?' on page 14, but what are you offering the individual in this particular post? What is there to aim at? A directorship when you go public?

This is not the same as the conditions of service. We are looking at the long term and it can be made clear that this will depend on market and other forces. You may well decide that none of this should appear in the written specification. So be it, but it is as well to have given the matter some thought so that questions from worthy candidates can be answered properly.

At the end of all this you will have the nearest thing to a blueprint possible when dealing with human beings:

- you know what you want
- you have the basis for the draft advertisement
- you can give an agency all it needs to know
- you have a framework on which to base your interviews
- you have the format for an offer of an appointment.

There are some very experienced personnel managers who maintain that a job specification should be brief; that it should never be more than, perhaps, two pages in length.

In a small to medium-sized firm, this can be dangerous advice. For one thing, as will be seen later, the job specification will become part of a contract and errors of omission can be costly when things go wrong. More important is the value of the full description at the interview. It is the basis of the structure of the whole meeting and provides every candidate with an equal opportunity to show where he or she fits the requirement. It also assists the interviewer to uncover deficiencies. Brevity in the job specification can mean that something will be overlooked and important questions left unasked.

It can also be true that a brief job specification indicates that every aspect of the vacancy may not have been considered before recruitment is started. That is all too often the cause of disaster.

Maybe you will think all this is going to take time. Yes, it is. Better to spend time now and get off on the right foot than to rush into expensive failure at a later stage. You want the best for your company. Surely that means you should take care.

Specimen job specification

This job specification is a version of that provided by the author acting as a selection consultant for a client.

BLOGGS PLASTICS LTD

address

The company was founded in 1946 by two brothers, William and Samuel Bloggs, when they left the RAF. They began in a very small works making plastic components for the textile machinery industry. Expansion in the 1950s was rapid and they were incorporated in 1957 as a private limited company.

William Bloggs died in 1965 and his brother, Samuel, continued as managing director. He was joined by his son Robert in 1980. Robert is now managing director. The father is chairman of the company, but is really semi-retired.

The company has a turnover of just over £2.5 million. It employs a total of about 220 men and women.

There has been particularly strong growth over the past five years in the export markets. Sales are mainly injection moulded plastic products for the engineering and electronic industries. Prospects for further expansion appear to be good provided some organisational and production problems are overcome. It is hoped that the appointment of a new works manager will further this end.

The job
The works manager will be expected to take full control of production departments.

Authority
1. The authority delegated to the works manager will be fully in accordance with the responsibilities and duties.
2. He will have full authority over all personnel in the factory. He will have power to recruit, transfer, promote and, within statutory limits, dismiss any employee, except in the case of senior appointments at third-line management. These cases will be subject to discussion with the managing director.
3. He will have authority to purchase any item of consumable stores and any immediate item of raw material within an agreed budget.
4. He will have authority to recommend to the managing director any capital item for inclusion within the accepted budget, but will be expected to justify his recommendations economically.

Responsibilities and duties

Responsibilities
1. The works manager will be responsible directly to the managing director.
2. He will be responsible for complete control of the organisation and of the profitability of every part of the factory.

Duties

1. To prepare a detailed production programme in association with the requirements of the sales manager, ensuring that customers' requirements regarding delivery dates are met.
2. To ensure that all production conforms to customers' specifications in respect of quality and quantity.
3. To prepare annual budgets for the factory covering all cost centres.
4. To investigate any costs which exceed budget and report details to the managing director.
5. To ensure adequate stock levels in relation to raw material, tools and finished parts.
6. To establish labour requirements to meet the production programme.
7. To investigate methods of payment and working hours. To submit proposals to the managing director prior to consultations with the trade unions – mainly the General, Municipal, Boilermakers and Allied Trades Union.
8. To ensure adequate quality control and constant review of inspection methods.
9. To maintain a continual review of all tooling problems and ensure that surplus tools are scrapped after consultation with the sales manager.
10. To ensure adequate maintenance of all plant and equipment.
11. To ensure that all goods leaving the factory are packaged according to customers' requirements.
12. To maintain security of all stocks, plant and buildings.
13. To ensure that all statutory requirements regarding health, safety and employment are met.
14. To develop all personnel and arrange adequate training.
15. To handle all industrial relations matters in consultation with trade union representatives particularly in relation to shift working.

Knowledge and experience

Essential
1. Some years' experience of works management in engineering.
2. Knowledge of modern management techniques and experience of applying them.
3. A sound engineering training.

Desirable
1. Experience of tool engineering.
2. Knowledge of injection moulding techniques.
3. Experience of working with a work force of mixed race.
4. Administrative experience.

General education
It is unlikely that the works manager will have the necessary technical qualifications without relevant O level passes. Adequate literacy and numeracy will be expected.

Technical education
The works manager must at least have served an engineering apprenticeship and will probably be a member of an engineering institution (mechanical, production or similar), although a lesser qualification may be considered if there is an adequate background of experience.

Compatibility
The works manager will have to maintain a harmonious relationship with the managing director, the sales manager and the design manager. There may also be contact with outside concerns such as sub-contractors regarding tools and with customers regarding quality of products and deliveries.

External activities
There will be no objection to any external activities unless they inhibit full dedication to the job in hand.

Age
It is unlikely that an applicant will have the level of experience

required until age 33. There is no relevant upper age limit.

Mobility
Some travel within the UK is likely and it will almost always be at very short notice. There may be occasional overnight stays. Foreign travel (at equally short notice) may also be possible – but rare.

Conditions of service

Period of notice.   Three months.

Service agreement.   None is envisaged at present.

Holiday entitlement. Six weeks plus statutory holidays. Considerable flexibility will be required since the factory usually works on bank holidays and the attendance of the works manager may be essential on occasion.

Sickness leave.   Any payment beyond statutory provision will be at the discretion of the board of directors.

Normal hours of work.   0800 to 1645 daily, but the factory is in production for 24 hours per day, 7 days per week. Flexibility on the part of the works manager is essential.

Salary.   Starting at around £18,000. A company profit-sharing scheme is planned for next year.

Pension scheme.   There is a firm's contributory pension scheme in operation with employee contribution of 5 per cent of gross salary. The normal retiring age is 65 and there is free life cover equivalent to one year's salary. This whole scheme is, however, under review in consultation with the firm's broker.

Expenses.   All out-of-pocket expenses will be reimbursed as they are incurred. It is not considered that a car is necessary in connection with this appointment but, whenever one is used, a mileage allowance in accordance with the latest Automobile Association rates for an 1800cc vehicle will be paid.

Relocation.   It is not expected that any relocation problem will arise, but assistance may be discussed with a worthy candidate.

Private health insurance.   A group scheme for private health insurance is in operation. Cover will be provided for the works manager who can include spouse and other members of the family at own choice.

Prospects
It is quite possible that the works manager could be appointed to the board of the company in due course, but there are no plans at present to increase the size of the board and no guarantee can be given at this stage.

Financial prospects will be in line with the progress made by the company and the contribution which the works manager has made to it, together with ability and acceptance of any additional responsibilities undertaken.

3
WHERE TO LOOK

With a carefully prepared and detailed job specification in hand, it is now time to decide where to look. There are a number of sources of recruitment and all have their place.

- In-house (see Chapter 10)
- Old Boy Network
- Agencies
- Executive selection consultants
- Executive consultants ('headhunters')
- Advertising

Old Boy Network

The OBN can be very risky and it will nearly always be slow. It is unlikely to produce more than one candidate at a time and, therefore, gives no real choice. There can be no harm in letting it be known round the golf club or similar points of contact that there is a job going. It is always possible that someone will have a relative who is 'just what you want'. Nevertheless, it has to be recognised that the individual who 'looks good socially' can be quite impossible to work with in business.

If the OBN produces a name or suggestion, make sure that the first approach is by an applicant (however tentative) and not the other way round. An accusation of 'poaching' by a competitor or neighbouring firm can be embarrassing. In any case, it is not for you to ask a person if he or she is interested in working for your company. That is a very different matter from telling someone that a job is vacant and saying that you are open to receive applications.

The sensible reaction, when approached, is to hand over an abbreviated job specification (maybe a copy of an advertisement) saying that if the contact is interested, you will be prepared to have a chat. This indicates that you are willing to consider an application. No more than two promises should be given:

1. To explain what the job is all about (ie go through the job specification).
2. To give all due consideration to that person's qualifications and experience.

It is perfectly reasonable to ask such a candidate to be patient until you have other people to consider. It is also perfectly reasonable to give a polite, but firm, rejection on the spot to the obvious misfit.

The OBN can be a good preliminary step in planning for a coming retirement. It can be a move in advance of advertising or the use of another source. To spread the word six months or even a year ahead of a need to recruit can produce a number of applicants worth seeing when the time for an appointment actually comes.

The OBN can sometimes put one at risk of offending one's friends. The regular bridge partner who 'knows about' your business from what you have told him in the past may be a little put out when you find that his nephew or niece is little more than a fool.

Agencies

The agency, unlike the consultant, will make a charge only when an appointment has been made. There is, therefore, no commitment on the client's part in letting a number of agencies have sight of the job specification. The modern one will almost certainly have a computer into which the requirements will be fed. It can, therefore, make sense to discuss the parameters so as to make sure that they have not been drawn too tightly. It has been known, for instance, for a specified lower age of 30 to exclude a 'paragon' of 29½ simply because the computer had no imagination.

The agency puts forward only those people who have registered with it and who are actually seeking new jobs. It offers no prospect of finding the man or woman who is working happily elsewhere, but who would jump at the chance of a new challenge if only it had been known to exist.

The management of the agency will probably have carried out a form of interview with all those on its register and there will, therefore, be an assessment in the print-out from the computer. But this will be general and have no reference at all to the vacancy. Thus, from the agency will come details which might be thought to be just a little better than letters in response to an advertisement.

If the agency can provide a good short list and choice, this is fine. Only in the particular circumstances at the time can a decision be made as to whether this source of recruits is the right one.

Which agency should be chosen? The Yellow Pages are full of names and, usually, give an indication of any speciality. Obviously, a firm which shows a leaning towards secretarial and clerical jobs will be unlikely to offer production managers, but others will. It will cost no more than a few telephone calls to find the right one (or two or three).

Finally, if that all-important job specification is lacking in any way, do not blame the agency for putting forward unsuitable candidates.

Executive selection consultants

It can be said that the job of the agency is to find jobs for people. The task of the selection consultant is to find people for jobs. At the same time, the aim is to provide the client with a good choice, based on detailed consideration of the client's needs, the job itself, and a full assessment of how closely each person on the short list meets the job specification.

Like the agency, the consultant will have a register of candidates, but it will usually be made up of people who have responded to previous assignments. There is little reason to believe that the man or woman you want has applied for another firm's vacancy. It can happen, but not often.

Consultants may be thought expensive. They are, unless one

thinks about the true cost of the time needed to do the job oneself. There can also be compensating advantages relevant to particular circumstances.

Look again at Chapter 1. The consultant has the advantage of seeing you as others see you. Maybe the initial consultation will help to avoid one of those costly mistakes.

From the outset, a good consultant will be prepared to help with preparation of that all-important job specification. He or she will know that the assignment will not succeed unless full information has been provided about every aspect of the vacancy and the firm. To that end, the consultation will involve very searching questions. Some of them will give the client cause for thought and may even change ideas. Nevertheless, there is never any question of the consultant knowing better than the client. It is his or her job, at this stage, to be sure that he or she has defined the need and, in particular, to be able to answer any questions which may be posed during the preliminary interviews.

Once the client has approved the job specification and, probably, drafts of advertisements, the assignment proper can begin.

With full confidentiality assured, a consultant will almost always attract those who would never write direct to a firm and, above all, would have a total distrust of box numbers. Every applicant knows it is possible to withdraw without the consultant's client ever knowing that he or she has applied. In the process, however, the consultant may have gained valuable information (see Chapter 6).

Most consultancy firms today use a personal details form rather like that set out in Appendix B. When a response to an advertisement arrives, a secretary will send the personal details form out at once. It is probable that the consultant sees applications only when there is a pile of forms. They can then be checked against the client's requirements. All those which approach a 'match' will be called to a personal meeting.

An interview by a good consultant will always be lengthy and detailed. A most careful assessment will also be written before any other person is seen. It is from the assessments that the short list is prepared. At no time, however, will a recommendation for an appointment be made or any attempt to 'sell' one candidate against others. The choice is always for the client to make alone.

As to timing, it is probable that, unless there are special circumstances, from consultation to short-list interview will take about six weeks. Much will depend on the particular job and, perhaps, the media used for any advertising.

Some clients object to the idea of the consultant producing only a short list. They want to see all the applications. They are fully entitled to do this so long as it is understood that there may be some withdrawals at first interview and those names must be withheld. It is, indeed, by no means unusual for a consultant to visit the client for a discussion about the assignment before a short list is drawn up.

Most firms of consultants today fix their fees as a percentage of the first year's salary attached to the job. Some potential clients find this objectionable. It is almost commercially unsound. A job to be filled at £25,000 a year at a company in the same town as the consultant's office must surely cost him less in time and travel than one a hundred miles away. For this reason, it makes sense to get a fixed quotation before giving an assignment.

It is also worth while asking to see some specimens of recent job advertisements. This will not only indicate the type and level of assignments which have been worked, but it also makes it possible to avoid the firm which tends to use media for self-advertisement. Nor should any copy appear to be 'selling' a job. Details given should be adequately factual and the display cost effective.

The price of space in the press will be added to the fee so it is worth while discussing the question of media selection before giving instructions. There is no point in full display in, say, the *Sunday Times* when semi-display in the *Bolton Evening News* will be adequate – or even better. The consultant is, nevertheless, entitled to justify his advice from past experience.

Executive search consultants

The popular name for the search consultant is 'headhunter'. Executive search is unlikely to be of service to the majority of smaller companies. It operates, usually, in a field where candidates are unlikely to respond to advertising or to put their names on agency lists. They probably never read the 'sits vac' anyway.

Like the selection consultant, the headhunter charges a

percentage of salary – but more so. At first sight, the fee may
sound horrific but, of course, there is no advertising cost.

Once the job specification is drawn up and agreed, the
headhunter starts to seek out possible candidates whom he can
approach. He will do this from office research and from
suggestions put to him by those he may think are 'in the know'.
Once he has a 'target' he will probably make a telephone call
saying who he is and seeking a meeting. It may be that he will be
quite open in asking if the 'target' is interested in the job or,
depending on the personality involved, he may be more oblique
saying he is seeking help and advice about whom to approach.

Either way, if there is interest, the target is then asked to apply
– in confidence, of course. After that, the process is just the same
as with the selection consultant.

As can be imagined, candidates for most of the jobs handled in
this way are the rarer kind. They are also difficult to approach and
tie down. It can, therefore, often take a long time for the short list
to be presented.

How to choose a consultant

In deciding to use a consultant (selection or search) one should
use three criteria:

- Can he show evidence of success in your kind of assignment?
- Is the individual consultant (not the firm) acceptable to you?
- In selection, is there evidence of cost-effective advertising?

Finally, one should always insist on the consultant appearing
when you meet the short list. There should be a ready willingness
to face the moment of truth. Something may go wrong. If it is his
or her fault, he or she should be there to recognise it so that it can
be put right. Perhaps the fault is yours (have you changed the job
specification without telling anyone?). If so, the consultant should
be present so that you can be shown what has happened.

Those who think consultants are a crazy idea should look at the
advertisements in the national and regional press almost every
day. The majority of management and professional vacancies are
placed either by consultants or personnel management and it is
striking that small to medium-sized companies seem to provide
the majority of the assignments handled by consultants. Someone

must be satisfied with their services. Maybe they are not for you, but they ought not to be dismissed without thought.

It is also worth noting that no sensible firm of consultants will be prepared to take on an assignment without any hope of success. It is not easy to reject business, but so much depends upon future recommendation by satisfied clients that undue risks will never be taken.

Such a refusal can give the prospective client food for thought and, at least, cause fresh consideration of what now appears as a management structure or other problem which must be solved before recruitment begins.

Advertising

Recruitment and advertising seem to go together in most people's minds. At one time, advertising was the most common way of proceeding. It is a very big subject. Copy prepared with care and skill and placed in the right medium can produce excellent results. But one should always seek quality in replies rather than quantity. A big response can suggest that the copy had room for improvement.

Someone once said that a correctly worded advertisement placed in the right publication should produce only one application – from the man or woman for the job. At least, that conveys an idea. Loose wording in the wrong place tends to bring too many letters which are utterly useless.

Space in the press today is expensive. There is no sense in wasting money, yet so many firms do just that.

The first step in recruitment advertising must be media selection. Will you advertise in:

- a national quality daily?
    eg *Daily Telegraph*
    The Times
    Financial Times
    Guardian
    Independent
- a popular daily?
    eg *Daily Express*
    Daily Mail

- a tabloid?
    eg *Sun*
       Daily Mirror
- a Sunday newspaper?
    eg *Sunday Times*
       Observer
       Sunday Telegraph
- a regional newspaper?
    eg *Birmingham Post*
       Manchester Evening News
       Leicester Mercury
- a periodical?
    eg *Economist*
       Spectator
       New Statesman.
- a trade or professional journal?

The list of possible choices seems endless. Three factors seem worthy of consideration:

- How quickly do you expect a response?
- Where is the person you want most likely to read your announcement?
- From how wide an area are you prepared to recruit?

Space taken in a trade or professional journal will have a good chance of being seen by most of those with the qualifications you are seeking. But when? Some set copy dates many weeks ahead of issue. Nor are these magazines studied with care the day they arrive on people's desks. It can often take months before you receive every last application. Of course, that very last letter can look most attractive. It is also annoying when the job was filled a couple of months earlier.

Perhaps one of the quality Sunday papers will claim with justice that most, say, chartered accountants buy it, but we know for certain that they all receive *Accountancy*. When they get round to it, they will read the small classified columns which will have cost a fraction of the price of the national newspaper. They could fail to look closely at their Sunday newspaper if the weather is good and the golf courses and gardens beckon.

If you are not prepared to pay removal expenses, this could be a sound argument against expensive space in a national newspaper when, say, the local or regional daily or evening press will bring in an adequate response.

Media selection is never easy and the firm which seldom recruits into management could well be advised to consult an advertising agency with a well-established 'classified' department. It will make no charge. The publishers pay a commission.

It can be wise to use a combination of newspapers and trade or professional journals. If so, timing needs careful coordination. Copy sent to a 'daily' may well appear next week, but the *Journal of the Society of Leather Technologists and Chemists* (according to *British Rate & Data*) requires copy six weeks ahead of issue. That publication also appears only six times a year.

The advertising agency can quote the likely cost and effectiveness of each medium. What matters to you is the price you must pay to reach an adequate number of qualified candidates. A panel of 5 cm across two columns in a national daily or Sunday paper costs as much as half a page in the *Chemical Engineer* or a quarter page in *Accountancy*.

Obviously, you should never waste time but, once again, it is stressed that what really matters is the best result in the long term – not the quickest.

After media selection comes preparation of copy and a decision regarding the space required. Go back to that all-important job specification. You now have to write a précis of it listing the main essentials – job title, place, salary, other benefits, and the qualifications and experience required. The classified manager at the advertising agency will be able to help if given the job specification to study.

Perhaps you will think of using a box number. Forget it. Would you be prepared to write to a totally anonymous body giving your personal details? Of course not.

A good advertising agency will offer a confidential reply service. With this, applicants can enclose a list of firms to which their letters may not be sent. This is perhaps just a little better than the use of a box number, but not much. The applicant still cannot be sure that a letter will be withheld from every possible undesirable adressee.

There can be good reason why a firm will wish to remain anonymous. Maybe it does not want a competitor to know it is recruiting. Perhaps the reason for the vacancy is not yet ready to be made known even to the existing staff of the company. Provided there is a strong case for anonymity, the only sensible course is to retain a consultant. There is never a good case to be made for the use of a box number and seldom one for the use of the confidential reply service.

Advertising copy should be designed to explain, as succinctly as possible:

- what the firm is
- where the job is
- what the job is
- what experience is needed
- what qualifications are
  - (a) essential
  - (b) desirable
- what the salary etc will be (if possible)
- what information is required in the response

The advertisement for the job with Bloggs Plastics described on pages 21-26 appeared in the *Daily Telegraph* and *Plastic & Rubber Weekly*. It read as follows:

WORKS MANAGER

For an expanding company situated at . . . manufacturing a range of plastic products for the engineering and electronic industries.

The salary will be in the region of £18,000 with other benefits intended to attract an ambitious chartered engineer. Relevant experience below the age of 30 is unlikely.

The works manager will report directly to the managing director and have full control of the factory. He will be expected to use modern management techniques and to improve efficiency and profitability. Knowledge of plastics tool engineering is desirable.

Please write with a full CV to . . . .

There were 48 applications which suggested loose wording. Ten had knowledge of tool engineering. This was a surprise and indicated that that point might have been advertised as 'essential' rather than as 'desirable'.

Apart from this criticism, note how the copy corresponds to the job specification. The salary was included and this is standard practice for the consultant who is not, at this stage, naming his client. When a company advertises for itself, there can be sound arguments for and against announcing a figure. Maybe one does not want competitors to know what one pays. Perhaps there are good reasons why the time is not ripe for other members of the management team to know what is in mind. Whatever the reason, whatever the copy may say, it is essential that it should convey the right impression. So many advertisements give cause for suspicion that either the salary will be so low that the firm is ashamed of it or that there is no real appreciation of what ought to be paid. One useful sentence is: 'Anyone earning less than £x at present is unlikely to have the experience . . .' This, at least, shows that the firm has some idea of the value of the job. It also indicates that there is a willingness to pay £x plus a considerable premium. Nevertheless, it is always best to name the salary whenever possible.

On the following pages are the texts of a number of advertisements taken from regional and national newspapers with comments. One is entitled to wonder what the success or failure rate was, but it is not hard to guess with a few.

The way in which the advertisement is drafted and presented will determine its response. Unless one has experience of artwork and printing design and layout, it really can pay to engage the expert – the advertising agent with a good classified department. From there, if nothing else, will come advice on:

- media
- timing
- type of advertisement:
    - (a) classified
    - (b) semi-display
    - (c) full display.

Every stage of recruitment and selection has its hazards and, once again, it has to be said that success can never be guaranteed. All one can do with certainty is to minimise the risks of failure. Skilful advertising can do a great deal towards that end.

The following advertisement (semi-display) appeared in a regional evening paper:

Experienced

PURCHASING OFFICER

required for progressive distribution company based in Blanktown near Elsewhere. Storage and distribution experience essential. Remuneration package according to experience.
Please apply box . . .

How much thought had been given to what is wanted here? Those who know Blanktown will recognise the firm anyway, so why use a box number? If not, the Yellow Pages for Elsewhere would soon reveal it. Was there something to hide? The copy, too, is full of 'nothing' words.

'Experience' and 'Experienced' are used three times. What does it mean? If experience is essential it ought to be possible to define it and name the salary. To leave it out suggests that candidates with different levels of experience will be considered. One suspects, however, that the firm really had no clue what it should pay and was hoping to recruit someone cheaply.

Perhaps the firm was satisfied with the response it got and, should its managing director see this criticism, he may say it is all poppycock. If so, he was lucky. The advertisement hardly suggests a happy firm and only those desperate for a job would apply.

The following was printed in the classified section of a national quality daily:

GENERAL MANAGER required for Japanese food importer and wholesaler. Must speak Japanese fluently. £12,000 per annum. Send CV to . . .

This is fascinating. Are we really to believe that the only qualification required of a general manager is fluency in an oriental tongue? In 1988 is £12,000 a realistic salary for one with quite a rare attribute *plus* some sort of undefined management ability?

Here is another (semi-display) from the same quality daily:

PRODUCTION
MANAGER

required for a . . . manufacturing firm in . . . Candidates should have ability to lead and motivate staff and have experience in the . . . or similar industry. Salary according to age and experience. Send CV to . . .

What age? What degree of experience? This suggests that the advertiser simply has not thought about producing a job specification and really does not know what is wanted. After all, to be facetious, experience in any industry could be as a senior manager or as the tea boy.

This is another semi-display the same day in the same paper:

CHIEF
EXECUTIVE

required for a small . . . company situated in . . . (county). Possible equity participation and salary negotiable. Previous experience in senior management necessary.

What is really wanted here? How chief and how executive? To whom will the new person report? A large, low-quality response is most likely. It will not 'pull' really senior people.

From a quality Sunday paper comes another semi-display:

EXECUTIVE PERSONNEL OFFICER

... Ltd, a fast expanding retail chain with over 500 employees, requires an experienced go-ahead person. Apply in writing to ...

What on earth is an 'executive' personnel officer? Is the job concerned with industrial relations (eg wages)? Is it a welfare officer's job? With what level of recruitment will it be concerned? One is prepared to bet that whoever received the applications would have a headache sorting them, but how many would be of the calibre required? Since the calibre is not stated, that is one of those good questions.

From a regional evening newspaper – full display:

BLANK & BLANK PLC

have a vacancy for a

WORKS SUPERINTENDENT

to manage and organise the assembly/fitting department.

This vacancy is suitable for a person with light mechanical or electrical experience, capable of controlling staff and organising production methods to achieve output and quality to programme.
Apply in writing to:
        General Manager (works) ...

What, one wonders, is a works superintendent? It does not look like a job in senior management because there is a General Manager (Works). Is the vacancy for a foreman? How many staff will the new person control? This advertisement could result in quite the wrong level of applicant. It would also be a help if the reason for the vacancy was given.

The advertisement below appeared as a full display in a quality Sunday paper:

PRODUCTION MANAGER

... Ltd is one of the fastest growing, privately owned companies in the UK. We have a product second to none, and our aggressive development programme will keep us in the number one position. Continued demand for our products and increased export effort mean that our production targets are becoming increasingly more difficult to attain. We are seeking a production manager with energy and enthusiasm to control and develop a small but extremely busy assembly unit. Responsible for production, procurement, stores and production engineering, you will report to the managing director and be allowed an autonomy which is seldom found in manufacturing today.

Ideally, you will be over 30 years of age, with an engineering background and a good working knowledge of computerised manufacturing systems. Sound man management skills are essential and the ability to communicate at all levels is required.

In return, we offer a negotiable salary, company car and all other benefits associated with a progressive company.

Send full CV to ...

Here is a good explanation of what is wanted and why. One is, perhaps, entitled to wonder why the salary figure in mind was not given, but it does suggest that the firm's managing director, to whom applications were to be sent, knew what he was about. Copy like this brings in the quality responses while acting as a deterrent to the faint-hearted. It certainly does not attempt to 'sell' the job as a cushy number.

GENERAL MANAGER
for
BUGSMOBILE DEALERSHIP

A golden opportunity has arisen to join a prestigious vehicle franchise as general manager.

The successful applicant will need to be self-motivated, confident, a strong communicator and, above all, experienced at this level. The generous package offered is by way of salary around £25,000 pa, a bonus, choice of Bugsmobile car (plus petrol and expenses) and 4 weeks' annual holiday.

Apply in writing with full CV to . . . Box Number . . . Evening Bugle, Blanktown.

This advertisement appeared in full display in a regional evening newspaper. Why a box number was used is a complete mystery. The paper concerned circulates only in a closely knit community. Everyone in the motor trade would, therefore, know at once which firm was advertising. Anyone else who was interested need only look at the *AA Handbook* and there is the name of the Bugsmobile dealer.

'Self-motivated', 'confident', 'strong communicator' – these are all words which really mean very little. We all think we have these qualities.

What a pity, too, that the copy does not say what is wanted. What about fleet sales? Type of market? What is the future? Why is the vacancy there? One can think of so many more questions which would be going through the minds of interested readers of that paper that evening. With just a little more thought, a much more sensible advertisement could have been drafted.

The only thing to be said in favour of the wording in the advertisement below is that every interested applicant would know who was going to read the response and would have some idea of what it was all about. It probably worked in spite of itself.

CHARNWOOD BRICK HOLDINGS LTD
WORKS MANAGER

Would you like to work for a small company renowned for its quality products and personal service?

If so, then we are looking for a works manager at our Leicestershire plant.

The successful applicant will be responsible directly to the MD for the profitable manufacture of our traditional handmade bricks. Considerable experience in, and enjoyment of, man management and clay technology are the essential qualifications.

Salary and benefits will be by negotiation and the job will include a company car.
Write in confidence with brief career details to: P J Clift, Charnwood Brick Holdings Ltd, Old Station Close, Shepshed, Leics LE12 9NJ

This advertisement is from the December 1986 edition of *Euroclay*, the journal of the Institute of Clay Technology. The cost (4 cm across two columns) at the time was £120. It stood on its own among editorial matter and would, therefore, be seen by virtually every member of the Institute – not only those actually seeking jobs. They would also know Charnwood well enough not to need a detailed description of the firm.

The snag, as has been said earlier, would lie in the timing. Latest copy date for this issue was 10 November and in fact applications, it is understood, were still arriving the following February.

Finally, a comment about age. This appeared in a national daily in full display.

FIELD SALES MANAGER

As part of our planned growth programme we wish to appoint a field sales manager to exploit the following brief:

- To manage, motivate and train our existing sales team, maintaining direct key customer contact and so leading by example.
- To secure a large number of new major accounts involving negotiations at director level.

You will probably be over 25, have proven ability in selling and want to move to a leader in the . . . market. First-year earnings c £20,000 are to be expected together with company car and full expense package. Applicants should send full CV to . . .

Assuming that anyone of 25-26 years of age can do all this, the advertisement says it all. But would it put off the 35+ men and women of the right experience and, perhaps, a more mature presence who would carry greater weight with the existing sales team which is to be trained, and also with those customers with whom negotiations are to be held at director level? Perhaps just a little less emphasis on the age (by saying something like 'at least 25 years . . .) might have been better.

4
MANAGEMENT FROM THE FORCES

In deciding where to look for managers, no company today ought to overlook the armed services and their agencies.

Back to Work in Civvy Street (written and published by Jim Henderson, Wilsontown, Forth, Lanark ML11 8ER) is a handbook for the guidance of those approaching the end of service in uniform. It lists no less than 135 companies keen to hear from all ranks. They recognise, if nothing else, that to have been accepted into the forces of today, men and women have undergone a rigorous selection procedure followed by a highly sophisticated development programme.

The qualities offered by service personnel

Academic and professional
All three services encourage the gaining of academic and professional qualifications in almost every discipline. Frequently, one hears of arts and science degrees having been acquired while with the colours.

Technical
Every service man and woman has the opportunity to acquire technical skill. It can range from mechanical, electrical or electronic engineering to the most sophisticated 'high tech' with membership of most of the professional institutions and societies. Each of the three services has its own training schools and there are very advanced courses at the combined services colleges. A science qualification from Shrivenham, for instance, carries considerable prestige.

Management

If any promotion has been earned – commissioned or not – it follows that there has been experience of getting the best out of others. In uniform, it is called 'leadership'; in civilian life, 'management'. It is, perhaps, this quality above all which leads Jim Henderson's 135 firms to look to the forces.

Some may ask what kind of numbers are 'managed' by officers and non-commissioned officers so that they might equate service skills with the requirements of commerce and industry. This is not an easy question to answer. A young subaltern, newly out of Sandhurst into his infantry regiment, is likely to be put in command of a platoon of some 30 men and be responsible for them and their equipment. A captain or major may command 150. A lieutenant colonel 750 to 1000. In another arm, however, the numbers will very different. In some cases, the young officer will be in charge of twice as many; in others, far less.

In recruiting from the forces, one needs to check career experience and qualifications as thoroughly as from any other source.

There will, nevertheless, hardly be a technical or academic qualification in industry or commerce which cannot be met from a service agency. Moreover, the qualification will almost certainly be combined with some management experience.

Loyalty

Those who have engaged management from service agencies refer continually to a peculiar brand of loyalty in both service men and women which engenders a desire to become established as a member of a team.

Some may, perhaps, express a doubt about this if they have not seen it at first hand. Can anyone with service experience, they ask, adapt to a commercial environment? There is the image of the retired colonel or sergeant major, happy to supplement a pension without working too hard.

This is to fail to understand what has happened since national service came to an end. Yes, there will be a pension, but the ex-service man and woman of today will still be young enough to have family responsibilities. Probably children will still be at school. There will always be a desire for a new career with a good salary and prospects, building on the foundations laid in the first.

Apart from the fact, therefore, that loyalty comes naturally in service life, there is every incentive to carry this through into the years ahead.

Age
There are ex-service personnel of all ages. The Officers' Association reports that jobs are found for commissioned ranks of anything from 26 to 57. Some leave in their mid-twenties after short service commissions while those who achieve the higher ('flag') ranks come on to the 'market' in their late fifties.

The Regular Forces Employment Association which deals with those from the non-commissioned ranks gives similar examples of placings over an even wider range. It is unlikely that a private soldier or equivalent, getting his discharge as soon as possible (maybe as young as 20) will have much management experience, but an ex-petty officer RN will have a great deal.

Planning
The 'regular' usually begins to plan the move into civil life as early as two years ahead. There are resettlement interviews, panels, boards and courses. As a result, there is often a job lined up and most will, in any case, have a good idea of the kind of new career they want.

Mobility
Partly as a hedge against inflation, it is likely that a house will have been bought during service so that families will be settled in a chosen location almost irrespective of job prospects. But this does not mean total immobility in the face of a good job offer. In the main, ex-service people are as mobile as their civilian counterparts.

There may be a preference for the south of England, but most non-commissioned ranks and some officers have found that property prices have made them look north and west. Thus, there are candidates available in all regions.

Sources of service recruitment

There are three main sources of recruitment from the forces and their principal addresses are given below.

The Officers' Association

The Officers' Association was formed after World War I. It is now run on the lines of an employment agency, yet it has some similarities with a consultancy. Ex-officers assess the potential, qualifications and interests of candidates in full and quite lengthy interviews. There are usually some 800 to 1000 men and women on the books and the Association claims about 300 placings in a year at home and overseas. Once a job specification has been received, a list of people for interview is drawn up and prospective employers can have full particulars within a few days. Interviews can be arranged quickly. Availability for a job will, of course, depend on whether the candidate is out of uniform yet.

The Regular Forces Employment Association

This organisation has 40 branches throughout the country. It exists to help those who have held non-commissioned rank (eg from private soldier to regimental sergeant major). In spite of its spread of offices, it is a small concern trying to do a big job on a tight budget. But when contact is made, there is an impression of considerable competence.

Corps of Commissionaires

Emerging in the field as a commercially oriented body is the Corps of Commissionaires. It still provides those worthy and impressive chaps who add dignity to reception areas and strike fear into the hearts of gate crashers at the members' enclosures of county shows. It now also offers a full employment agency service for anyone who has held non-commissioned rank in any of the three services, police or fire brigades. It has a growing reputation as a source of recruitment for a variety of management posts but, unlike the other two bodies, it makes a charge of about 10 per cent of the first year's salary when an appointment is made.

The literature and reports of all three organisations show jobs filled with success in almost every branch of management and level of qualification. While candidates for every possible vacancy can never be assured, it is always worth while offering them sight of every vacancy. You never know, perhaps you will be seeking an accountant the very day a senior officer retires from the Royal Army Pay Corps or perhaps you will find a warrant officer from the Royal Army Ordnance Corps is available for that stores management job you have vacant.

All three organisations agree that they are more likely to be able to work efficiently if they have sight of a full job specification.

Addresses

The Officers' Association, 48 Pall Mall, London SW1Y 5JY; 01–930 0125

Regular Forces Employment Association, Head Office, 25 Bloomsbury Square, London WC1A 2LN; 01–637 3918

The Corps of Commissionaires, Head Office, 3 Crane Court, Fleet Street, London EC4A 2EJ; 01–353 1125

5
DECIDING WHO TO INTERVIEW

Few things are more daunting than a massive pile of job applications. In theory, it should never happen. A correctly drafted job specification followed by a well-presented advertisement or handled by the right agency should produce only a few worthwhile replies. But we saw what happened to the response to the vacancy at Bloggs Plastics (page 36). In practice, too, there will always be the folk who will go for 'the long shot' – a job they have no right to expect. In addition, there will probably be some 'near misses' who think they might have a chance.

Sorting applications

That pile has got to be tamed. How? First, every letter should be checked against the job specification:

- Does it show *all* the essential qualifications?
- Does it indicate the essential level of experience?
- Does it give you *exactly* what you asked for in the advertisement?

It is a cause of constant amazement that so many people who are supposedly anxious to impress a prospective employer seem unable to read an advertisement properly. You ask for age; why is it omitted? Why are only very brief details given when you asked for a full CV? You asked for a career summary; why have you been sent a ten-page life history.

When this happens, you can be excused for thinking there is a sloppy mind incapable of absorbing simple instructions. What would that mind do to a request from a customer? On the other hand, some particular such as age may be left out because there is a need to hide it. You can only judge for yourself and decide whether the 'transgression' is important.

From this first perusal, you should be able to make two piles:

- possibles
- hopeless.

Get that hopeless lot out of the way at once. Send a duplicated (if necessary) letter to say the application has been studied, but that you regret that the levels of experience and qualification do not appear to match the need as well as those of a number of other applicants.

Now, re-check the possibles more carefully against that job specification and with particular reference this time to the 'desirable' requirements. You may take the view that those which fail to show all the 'essentials' should be rejected. Yet you may feel more lenient to one who has a number of 'desirables'. A consultant with your instructions in mind is likely to reject at once.

Personal details forms

There are some who believe the best way of sorting is to have a personal details form completed by everyone – irrespective of what is in the original letter. Indeed, many personnel officers no longer ask for letters of application but, in their advertisements, say, 'Please apply for a form.'

The advantage of this is that it puts everything in precisely the same order from everyone. Thus, the forms are more easily checked against the specification.

Another advantage of the form is that it will almost invariably be in the applicant's own handwriting and this can be compared with the original letter. Everyone is entitled to expect a candidate for a job to take time and trouble over presentation of a letter which he or she hopes will appeal to a prospective employer, but with the typewritten offering, one can never be sure that it is all his or her own work. There are a number of organisations which will draft CVs and, indeed, write and produce letters on word processors. It would be wrong to condemn anyone for making the most impressive approach possible, but you need to get to the facts in choosing an important member of your management team.

There are others to whom forms smack of bureaucracy. They hate them on principle. There is, therefore, only one recommendation. The right way is the one which suits you. If you feel inclined to use a form, a suggestion is given in Appendix B.

Telephone contact

However you have done it, you should now have an idea about which candidates you want to meet and it may still look a formidable task to have to give enough time to everyone. Herein lies a danger. You may just miss someone really good because of something in (or left out of) a letter. The answer is a preliminary telephone call.

There will almost always be a home telephone number on applications. A few hours on one or two evenings or at a weekend can be time well spent in preparing your interview list.

Do remember that the recipient of your call will be totally unprepared and 'off guard'. Begin, therefore, by checking that the call is no embarrassment. No one can talk easily about a future career in front of a bridge party or if the children are screaming for a bed-time story. Worst of all, think of the situation where the present employer is in the room. Start by asking if it is all right to speak just now or whether a later call would be preferred. At this stage, make it clear that you want only monosyllabic answers:

- Is it convenient for me to speak now?
- Would you prefer me to call in an hour or so? Perhaps tomorrow?

Once you are free from restraint, explain that this is no more than a preliminary contact to see if an interview is worth while. You have had a big response. You do not want to leave anyone out yet you cannot see them all. You can also add that it is always possible that, having heard from you, the candidate might want to withdraw anyway.

The main object is to start a two-way conversation. Ask if there are any questions. Check some detail in the CV. Ask if there would be any travel problems; if it will be convenient to come for interview at any time of the week etc. You want to hear as much as you can of the voice at the other end of the line and gain an impression of personality.

Everyone who has any experience of interviewing knows how some people whose written presentation has been excellent can turn an interviewer off within minutes of first personal contact. This preliminary telephone call can achieve the same end. Do allow for the fact, however, that the initial call will be a surprise and one deferred to avoid embarrassment will have been prepared for.

During the call you will be making notes from which you will prepare your short list. There will be cases in which someone will be so attractive that a date for a meeting can be made on the spot. This will be rare and invitations will normally be issued later.

As soon as all the calls have been made, letters of invitation should go out and actual face-to-face meetings held as soon as possible.

Those rejected should also be told they will not be seen.

This chapter describes a most important stage in the selection process. You cannot afford the time to see a large number and interview them thoroughly, yet neither can you afford to miss anyone who is worth a chance. The procedure described here has been tried and proved. It goes a long way towards reducing the chance of failure and yet eliminates the waste of time on hopeless cases.

In selecting candidates for interview, one needs to take care that there is no risk of accusation of discrimination on grounds of sex or race. ('I have all the qualifications, but I was not invited to interview because I am a woman/black.')

The preliminary telephone call can be an insurance against this. It will show that consideration was indeed given and all the qualifications taken into account.

Chapter 14 deals more extensively with the risks of discrimination charges.

6
WHAT IF NO ONE APPLIES?

In Chapter 5, some ideas were put forward for dealing with a big response to advertising. A much more worrying problem arises when there are no replies at all or none worthy of consideration.

This does happen even when all the possible agencies have been trawled and a fortune spent on advertising in a wide range of media. All too often it is assumed that there is a scarcity of people with the right qualifications or experience unless ridiculously high salaries are offered.

Never jump to conclusions. It is easy to mislead oneself, but it is vital that the whole truth (however disconcerting) is uncovered. It could be something so serious that the firm's future may be at stake.

Two reasons only

You have followed the advice given in earlier chapters? You have been looking in the right place and have not been expecting, say, to find a saggar maker in Wigan rather than Stoke-on-Trent? Then there can be only two reasons why your response is so poor:

1. There really is a shortage of people with the background you need.
2. There is something wrong (or thought to be wrong) with the firm or, let it be said, with the person who is advertising.

Until the cause is established beyond all reasonable doubt, it is no use pouring good money after bad with more advertising, higher salary offer, new perks or anything else.

If you have consulted the agencies and they have no likely candidates on their books, you have some prima facie evidence of a shortage. Look then at the jobs advertised in the press – particularly in your own region. Does it appear that there is an abundance of similar vacancies with the copy growing ever more enticing? If so, you have a management problem which you may be advised to solve by means other than recruitment. Look again at that job specification. Can it be changed? Could you, for instance, get along with HND instead of BSc? Would just a little less experience be adequate? Could a solution to your overall management deficiency be met by re-writing the job specifications of other people? Perhaps you have already decided against internal promotion. Could you think again? Perhaps there is a 'temporary' interim solution. Read Chapter 9.

'I would not work there because . . .'

What do you do if you are forced to admit that other firms can find the sort of person you want and it looks as if only you are missing out? There must be something wrong with your image. What is it? What is worse, does the image have substance? There are folk out there who are saying, in effect, 'I would not work there because . . .'. You have got to find the end of that sentence.

Some years ago, a famous multinational corporation had been advertising for trainee cost accountants. It needed six for its Manchester factory. After two advertising shots without any response, the personnel manager, in desperation and under pressure from the chief accountant, tried a box number. He knew this was seldom much use, but the company had problems. This time it did pull in three replies and all, however unsuitable they looked, were invited for interview. None of them turned up and none would say why. Two did go as far as to say they had decided not to seek a change. Under pressure both 'hung up' when asked if this was after knowing the name of the company.

This made the personnel manager send for a consultant who advertised with the usual promise of confidentiality. He obtained ten applicants who were all invited for interview. It was when the applicants were face to face with the consultant at his office that the name of the client was revealed for the first time and all sought to withdraw. But they were in the room and the consultant was thus able to get at the truth. It was widely believed, it appeared, that the Manchester factory was to close and everyone from there moved to work at Skelmersdale New Town. No Mancunian wanted to go there. (Maybe no one from 'Skem' wanted to move to Manchester, but that is not the point.)

In fact, the opposite was the truth. More cost accountants were needed in Manchester to cope with the increased load which would be caused when the Skelmersdale plant ran down and some of the production was moved to Manchester. The reason trainees were sought rather than fully qualified people was that the whole move would take some years and the development would give a valuable training period.

The consultant felt he had earned his fee by getting at that truth and enabling the firm to kill a harmful rumour.

This example may sound silly, but it is perfectly true. It can be argued that the rumour could have been scotched by a revision of the advertising copy. Of course it could – when it was known. All sorts of rumours can be spread about a firm without senior management knowing about them.

In this case, the consultant was retained for a full assignment to get at the facts. There may be less expensive ways, but the use of a box number will never be one of them.

The confidential reply service

In Chapter 3 reference was made to the confidential reply service offered by some advertising agencies and it was not recommended. There is, however, an exception to this rule. Faced with the 'no reply' situation, it can possibly be of some value. If your company's name appears frequently in the 'stop list', your agent can surely try a few telephone calls. He cannot give you names – it is a confidential service, after all – but he can ask for the reasons. If the same thing comes from a number of people, you will have the answer. It may, however, be that the replies will be evasive and, of course, your name will have been revealed – if that matters.

The agencies

If the agencies who have had your job specification have met refusals to allow particulars to be given to you, they must have asked why. Again, however, the answers could tend to be evasive.

Professional bodies

Professional institutions and societies with branches in your town or area will probably be prepared to comment on the availability of members. Some, indeed, have employment agencies. They are always worth asking for help and advice.

In situations such as the one described for cost accountants, there should be little difficulty in putting things right, but there can be more fundamental causes for concern.

The consultant discovers the truth

There was the managing director of a dye works who called in a consultant to advise on what could be done in the 'total absence' (his words) of dye house managers. He said he had advertised several times; offered 'no end' (his words again) of fringe benefits and still had no response. Thus was he convinced that there were no decent people around. He had used the name of the company and then box numbers. It made no difference.

The consultant had his suspicions, but kept his counsel. He asked to see the advertisements. They were identical in every case except for the salary, name or box number. The medium used was also the same every time. It really looked as if the 'handwriting' was being recognised. The misgivings of the consultant began to be justified.

For this reason, a proposal was made that the vacancy would be advertised as usual, but the assignment would proceed only to first interviews. After that, a further meeting and discussion would be sought. It was made clear that there was no thought of a short list being produced and the object was to diagnose the reason for past failures. The client agreed with some reluctance as he remained convinced that dye house managers of any worth simply did not exist any longer. Anyway, the 'dogsbody' who had left had been poached from him by a competitor. How the consultant wished he could meet that 'dogsbody'!

The usual procedure was followed and no less than six very interesting applications were received. All these people were invited to come to interview. It was then that the consultant's gut feeling was confirmed. No self-respecting dye house manager would dream of working for *that* firm with *that* managing director. He was impossible. He allowed no initiative; he gave no credit where it was due; he was, in effect, a bully. It appeared that he had had a number of good people in the past who had all moved on as fast as they could. In a small, closely knit industry such as that, reputations spread like a bush fire.

The consultant now had the task of telling his client the truth. All he could offer to do was to carry out a survey of the management structure of the firm with a view to re-arranging job specifications in the hope that the dye house could be controlled by existing personnel. This might have allowed the managing director time to recover his and the firm's reputation. Alas, the end of this story is now known. The consultant was shown the door. The anecdote is told in order to stress that an absence of applications does not necessarily indicate a shortage of the right people. The fault may lie with the firm and, until the real reason is known, there is no point in surmise. To act without proper information can cost money to no purpose.

7
FACE TO FACE WITH CANDIDATES

There is no shortage of advice about interviews and interviewing techniques. Courses and seminars abound; new ideas and gimmicks emerge and then fade away. Busy people whose main interests lie in other directions have neither the time nor the inclination to study the subject in depth. Nor should it be necessary for them to do so.

Obtain information

It is important to remember that in the space of an hour or two, you are going to have to provide yourself with enough information for a decision on whether the man or woman on the other side of the table is right for the job you want to fill. That decision is going to be of enormous importance to you and to your company or department – maybe for years ahead.

So far there has been careful preparation for this stage, but it is at interview that the success or failure of the entire recruitment and selection process is most at risk. It will help if you realise two things:

- Many candidates today have been well schooled in the art of selling themselves at interview.
- Some interviewers, lacking a complementary skill, put good candidates off and lose the best applicants because of the way they present themselves.

Basic rules

Everyone has a different personality and their own way of doing things. No one, therefore, can say exactly how you should conduct an interview. You have got to do it your way or appear in an artificial light. There are, nevertheless, five basic rules worth following:

Interviews must always be free of interruption

Telephone calls and knocks on the door can be confusing for both parties. Do remember that the person before you may be a colleague – even a partner – for years to come and must be worthy of your undivided attention. If your office is always like Charing Cross station in the rush hour and you cannot guarantee peace and quiet in working hours, hold the interviews when everyone has gone home.

Interviews should never be rushed

How long an interview should take depends on several factors. Some types of vacancy need more time than others. Marketing and sales may call for a probe into knowledge of customers and contacts. To uncover all this might well take several hours. Administration, accounts and personnel may mean a relatively simpler check on qualifications and experience; production, upon a knowledge and experience of an industry's techniques and methods. The only advice relevant to this is to give yourself ample time. It will always be better to have too much of that rather than too little.

Always interview at the place of work

To invite applicants to meet you at hotels or anywhere else away from the factory or office suggests there is something you want to hide. It is human nature for everyone to see where the job will have to be done. So, even if you are meeting out of office hours, do so on your premises. Yes. Perhaps you will have to ask a receptionist to work late – even pay overtime. So what? You are doing something which is worth doing properly and with care.

It can be that a sales executive will seldom see head office. It can then be simple common sense to have a preliminary chat 'on the territory'. There is nothing in this to alter the principle. A good area sales manager will expect to see the products, production and methods before accepting the offer of a job anyway.

Never try to sell the job or the firm

Every candidate whom you see – let it never be forgotten – is as free to reject the offer of a job as you are to make it. The firm is all-important to you, but to get the best result from all this, always let the facts speak for themselves. If you have been having a rough time, explain it and show how you plan to make things right; how this appointment has a part to play in the recovery.

Never start to interview without enough preparation

Plan in advance the main questions you want to ask. Put them on paper and never overlook any of them. If nothing else, this will ensure that you cannot be accused of discrimination (see Chapter 14). These questions should be drawn up with reference to the job specification and also to all the applications. In this way, you can be ready to compare one with another at decision time. If, for instance, one application lays stress on some particular knowledge or experience yet none of the others mention it, it can be a good idea to ask everyone about that point if it is of interest to you.

Six stages of interview

Within these basic rules, every interview, irrespective of the job or its level of importance, should pass through six stages.

Explain what the job is all about

There are two schools of thought about this first stage. You can either:

1. leave the candidate in reception for 15–20 minutes with the job specification, or
2. go through the whole thing verbally at the beginning of the meeting.

The first method makes sure the full picture has been seen; that the candidate has had a real opportunity to study it and prepare questions. The other allows the interviewer time to study the facial expressions as the various aspects of the job and the firm are revealed.

Once again, the best way is the one which suits you so long as you adopt the same procedure with each candidate. To change during the process from one candidate to another must make the final assessments more difficult.

Ask for questions

No matter which way you carry out the first stage, it should be followed by, 'Do you have any questions?' Your object now is to start a discussion in which the candidates will be leading. There is hardly a better way of drawing out a personality.

The answer 'No' can be disappointing. It will suggest that little or no homework has been done. To turn up without any preparation is hardly impressive. At the very least, there should be evidence of knowledge of what the firm does, its markets, its size, its reputation. Candidates' questions ought now to reveal this. Maybe 'research' has been no more than a visit to the local library. ('In your specification you say you are giving a service to the . . . industry. Kompass Register does not refer to this. Is it something new?')

Even if the candidate has no questions, surely there is some comment even if you have to drag it out when you have a feeling that it would be unfair to cut the meeting short. You can enquire about knowledge of the company. This will depend on the kind of vacancy under consideration. A marketing and sales oriented person might be expected to know something about the competition and how it regards your firm. You would expect this to come naturally. A production controller might be different.

There is something to be said for the fact that an applicant who turns up totally 'cold' lacks interview training and you will not be facing a hard 'self-sell'.

Probe that CV

By discussing the firm as you have been doing until now, you have also, probably, done a great deal to put a candidate at ease. You can now turn the conversation round.

The particulars provided with the application or by the agency may be skeletal. Perhaps you asked for that anyway. It is now time to put as much flesh on the bones as you can. Start with the most recent job and work backwards until you have drawn out every necessary detail.

- What did you do?
- What did that mean?
- How did you do it?
- How big was the firm?
- How many people in your department?
- Who reported to you?
- To whom did you report?
- Why did you leave/why are you seeking a change?

These will be questions you have prepared in advance and it is going to be your only chance to get at the truth, free of embellishment and lacking no particular. Do remember that training may have been given in how to set out that CV, how to present past experience and how to be interviewed. A very junior role in a team effort with an outstanding achievement can sometimes be presented by the interviewee as if he or she had been the moving spirit.

I can recall the girl who conveyed the impression that she had played a major and significant role in a design team for a highly successful fashion range launched by a competitor of the firm at which she was being interviewed. The truth was that she had been a very junior draughtswoman following the specific instructions of a chief. She had neither shown nor been required to show any initiative. This emerged during a very careful and searching interview. Somehow, the dates had not seemed to fit the age, but this was not obvious from the start. In fact, later experience was proved to be more relevant, but her 'over-selling' nearly lost her the job instead of helping her cause.

One would be very impressed by someone who could claim to have worked with Alex Issigonis in the design of the original mini, but it would still be wise to know the exact capacity of the relationship. Was it at the right hand or in the canteen?

Even though you are now asking the questions, you are still aiming at discussion. Try not to draw monosyllabic answers. Always, 'How did you?' rather than 'Did you?' 'What do you think about . . .?' rather than, 'Would you . . .?'

You want to know how closely that person in front of you fits that job specification, but there is something more. In breaking down any barrier of diffidence, over-confidence, interview training or anything else, you have been trying to assess whether you are looking at a face which will fit. This is vital and yet there is really no way of describing in writing what you want.

Check compatibility

'Do you think you could work with me?' That is a perfectly fair question. From the way it is received you might get a clue as to whether you are wasting your time. For the last hour or so, you have been wondering whether you will offer a job to this one. The converse will also have been in the other mind. Maybe you would be surprised by a blunt rejection just at this moment, but any answer will be revealing. If there is any hesitancy, you have been warned (see Chapter 8). Maybe you would prefer to ask, 'If you are offered the job, will you accept?' The object – and almost certainly the result – will be the same.

These questions are not a ploy. They are designed to give the candidate a chance of clearing up any doubts about you and they should lead to a friendly chat about the 'atmosphere' of the job.

That last question

Before a candidate leaves, it is usual for the interviewer to give a chance to a candidate for final questions. If the meeting has been well organised and conducted, few are likely, but be prepared for: 'There is just one last question. Do you have any doubts about my ability to do this job?'

If you are not ready for it, this question can set you back. There is at least one very reputable firm in London which specialises in teaching redundant executives how to sell themselves into jobs. The question comes from there. The idea is to put the candidate into the driving seat at the end of the meeting. It is hoped that the answer will be some sort of semi-commitment, leaving room for a follow-up. It also provides, perhaps, for a final sales pitch. How you answer depends on your feelings, but there can be no harm in letting it be known you have heared the question before and know its origin. It is always fair to point out that you have a number of others to see and that you are not at present in a position to answer. This is also a good time to hint at the possibility of a second meeting.

Assessment

The interview is not over when you shake hands. Before you do anything else, make your assessment against the job specification. It can be on rough paper and in pencil if you wish. It is for your eyes alone, but it must be in writing. The assessment does not compare one individual with another. It compares the body who has gone out of the room with your idea of what you want. It is suggested that it be made under several headings which you will have decided are relevant, such as:

- personality
- work attitude
- qualifications
- experience
- knowledge etc.

If you can, see all the candidates the same day. This may not be possible and so the assessments in writing become even more important. They do help to avoid the dangers arising from tricks of memory. Some consultants, interviewing for clients, include a personal description (bald head, blue eyes, large ears). Some even take polaroid photographs.

A possible form for use in making assessments is set out in Appendix C.

What about diplomas?

Consultants are often asked if they will check on the truth of claims to professional or academic qualifications. It is seldom done, but there is no reason against it. There can never be any harm in asking for the production of certificates and the like. The letter of invitation can be phrased so that no hint is given as to doubt of the veracity of a claim.

It is always possible to check membership of professional institutes. Lists are published and can be seen in public libraries. For this reason, false claims are rare – and stupid. Things like HND and City and Guilds qualification are more difficult. Pieces of paper, however, are always available if you ask to see them. Do so if you will be happier.

Two interviewers?

Maybe you have a colleague (co-director, partner or other senior executive) whose judgement you trust. This is fine. Two heads are always better than one, but it is usually wise to hold two separate interviews, planned so that each interviewer will tackle the aspects of the job most suited to him. There should also be two completely independent assessments so that notes can be compared at the end of the process. It will then be possible to have a discussion and a joint selection.

The second opinion can be of particular value when you are selecting outside your own work experience. You may have a leaning towards one part of the management structure and be seeking help in another. If you are production or design minded and are seeking sales management, you may find it helpful to hear another view even if the colleague is, say, an accountant and as inexperienced in sales as you are.

The second look

Perhaps there is now only one candidate who seems to measure up adequately to your job specification. Certainly, if things have gone as they should have done, there ought to be no more than two. Perhaps the qualifications and experience are there, but are you equally confident about compatibility? Now is the time for a second look. Invite each candidate to a social occasion with wives and husbands. It may be lunch or dinner at a hotel or restaurant. Yes. It is going to cost time and money, but what are a couple of nights out when you are dealing with the future management of that important firm – yours?

It is not recommended that more than one candidate should be invited at a time. That is the way to disaster since it puts up barriers which you are trying to break down. If there was any evidence of skill or training in self-sell at the first meeting, the social occasion should enable you to tear through it.

Draw spouses into the conversation while making it clear beyond doubt that only the candidate is being selected. There should be no great need to go into detail about the job again. Your main idea is to find out about compatibility and, above all, to get an opinion from your own spouse who is the one person on whom you ought to be able to rely for utter frankness. 'That man will drive you up the wall in no time' can be such a useful remark.

With the spouse present, it is also a golden opportunity to clear up any doubts about such things as mobility and availability to travel at short notice without running into the sort of trouble described in Chapter 14.

It is fairly common practice for a job offer to be made at this second meeting. Such is not recommended. Take time for counsel with your pillow – sleep on it. A telephone call next day will make much more sense. In any case that 'helpful' remark from your spouse is more likely to come in the bedroom or at breakfast than at the restaurant.

What about references?

Should you seek references? If so, when? How? When and how should they be taken up?

The very last thing you need is the written platitude about honesty, punctuality, loyalty, conscientiousness and the rest. If you need assurance that there will be no dipping in the till, would you not be better off with an assurance fidelity bond? The value of a reference is what it tells you about a person's work and ability rather than the character on which anyone's ideas must be subjective. You have delved into the career history and yet you think that, somehow, you have less than the full story. Did that fellow really devise the new production method? Can that woman really sell those clothes?

A chat on the telephone with a referee can help so long as that referee is in a position to know the truth. There are always those who will say something on the telephone which they would never put in writing. Moreover, the *way* that something is said can be a real help.

Imagine how you might react when asked for a testimonial on a former employee if you were posed with this question: 'If he or she applied to you for a job now would you take him or her back?'

Would you put your answer to that one in writing? On the telephone, you might just be a little more forthcoming – if only in your tone.

You will never, of course, approach a referee without permission. This being so, why ask for names until you need them? Does not that suggest that the best time is at the end of a good first interview or even during the second?

It is common practice to offer a job, subject to satisfactory references. But what happens if the testimonials prove unsatisfactory?

Some local authorities issue forms to former employers after a new recruit has started work. This always strikes the recipient as rather strange.

No one will knowingly put forward referees who are likely to say the wrong things and only those about to be made redundant will name existing bosses. It is surprising how many quite senior and experienced managers seem to think that the local vicar is a good name. Unless, of course, he has been the employer, or has reason to be able to assess a work situation, do not accept this. Make it clear that you want the name of a person who has knowledge of work history at some recent stage of the career.

Husbands and wives

Nothing in the above should be taken as a recommendation that husbands or wives of candidates should actually be interviewed. That was a gimmick of the 1950s and 1960s and has been shown to be absolute nonsense. The whole idea is to make the meeting informal and, above all, to allow your own spouse to join you in making a personality assessment of the candidate.

The following (true) anecdote will illustrate the fatuity of what is now an 'old hat' idea.

A company in the Midlands had a vacancy for a London manager who would be important in fostering a large part of the turnover, particularly in exports. It was the 'in' thing at the time to interview wives. (Today it would have to be spouses. This was before the days of the Equal Opportunities Commission.) The company, therefore, insisted that all applicants should come for interview with their marriage partners.

The man who got the job produced a girl who was too good to be true. She was charming and demure with all the right social graces. The appointment was a great success and within a year the man had a seat on the board.

Shortly after this promotion, there was an exhibition at Earls Court where the firm had a stand and a social function was arranged for overseas buyers to which all wives were invited. The London manager, now director, came alone and explained that his wife was ill. Two years later, the same thing happened.

This time the managing director's wife went to the home out of sympathy. There she learned that the wife was a permanent invalid and had not been out of the house for about ten years. The woman at the interview had been from an escort agency. The man had wanted the job. He knew he could do it and was not going to lose the chance because his wife, to whom he was devoted, happened to be an invalid.

The story had a happy ending. The managing director congratulated the husband on his initiative and said he had proved himself in the job. He also told the board that wives would never be interviewed again.

8
TIME FOR DECISION

You have carried out all the interviews with meticulous care. You have compared your assessments with the job specification and, finally, with each other. You have discussed the whole exercise with your colleagues. It is time for a decision.

Are you going to make an offer?

You are, of course, in a very human situation and will never find the match which is perfect in every detail. There will be something lacking in every candidate you have seen. What you hope is that from all you have been doing will emerge a man or woman who is going to be a valuable member of the management team for a long time to come. Can you be satisfied beyond all reasonable doubt that you have met that person?

Of course, you have an urgent need to fill that vacancy, but unless you consider the risk of failure to be minimal, do not proceed. Far better to take time to think again than to live to regret what you have done. Consider, in the light of this experience if, perhaps, it might be better to use a different recruitment method or even amend that job specification and start again.

Let us assume you decide to proceed.

Telephone

There is now no point in delay. Speak to your choice on the telephone as soon as you can do so without risk of embarrassment. You need now to be as sure as you can be of acceptance. Do remember that just as you have been exercising your right to choose, so have all the people you have met. Anything could have happened to put them off. Your spouse, as we have seen, may have set you in doubt about the personality of one candidate. So may another spouse have done the same with you. Whatever the cause, if you are going to be spurned, you need to know now – not by return of even first-class post – and do remember that awkward people seldom worry about quick responses.

Avoid procrastination by a candidate

Some applicants can be utterly exasperating when they have an offer. The following exchange is by no means uncommon:

Employer: 'Thank you for coming to see us. I am calling to offer you the job. Will you be able to start on . . .?'
Candidate: 'Thank you. Can I think it over and let you know?'

The reasons for this kind of thing are many. There is at least one organisation advising redundant executives that no commitment is ever made until a job offer is accepted; that it is good for morale to receive offers and it is fair game for employers to be tagged along. Moreover, there may be more than one job in prospect. A bird in the hand may be worth two in the bush, but if it is possible to delay acceptance until the result of another interview is known, so much the better.

Whatever the reason, hesitation in the face of an offer can be disconcerting as anyone who has experienced it will confirm – and so many have. It puts the employer on the spot. Where does one go from here? An offer has been made and a hand has been shown. Yet now there is doubt and, if the selection has been a close run race, there may be a tinge of regret. Ought the offer to have been made to the runner-up?

To avoid this, always leave room for a tactical withdrawal. The following approach is recommended:

Employer: 'Thank you for coming to see us. I am calling to make certain that you are still interested in the job and to ask if any further questions have occurred to you since we met.'

In nine cases out of ten, this will bring a positive response, but any vacillation can be followed by:

'If I were to offer you the job, would you accept and be prepared to start on . . . as we discussed?'

(This can be a good time to ask if referees can be approached. The hesitating candidate may be thus led to show a hand.)

An approach on these lines keeps the employer in command of the situation. The least sign of indecision can be probed. You can ask what the problem is and you are also in a position to put on some pressure by indicating that the appointment has now to be made without delay; that a final decision will be made within 24 hours (less if you wish); that if you do not hear within that time limit, you will assume withdrawal. Your attitude will depend entirely on how you now feel towards this applicant and also, probably, on whether there is a good runner-up. Pressure now will act as a counter against the possibility that there is another in mind.

Some will think all this is laboured, but this will be only until the awkward character is encountered. Never think 'it can't happen here'. All too frequently, it does.

Appointment letter

Immediately there is a verbal acceptance, a confirming letter should be sent. It should:

- set out in detail all the terms agreed
- enclose a copy of the job specification
- fix a starting date
- demand an immediate return of a signed duplicate as acceptance of all the terms and conditions.

Only when that duplicate is back in your hands should you tell all the other applicants that the job is filled. The risk of refusal is now minimal, but it does happen. It still makes sense to retain an option to think again. Except in a photo-finish, one is unlikely to be satisfied with what might be regarded as second best, but there is no harm in retaining the right to have another look – however forlorn the hope may be.

Where there has been a difficult choice between two candidates, it can be worth going through the final telephone routine with both. Any hesitation on the part of one of them and keen interest from the other might be just what is needed to tip the balance. No offer has been made until you have what amounts to a verbal acceptance.

The whole process of recruitment and selection, from preparation of the job specification to these telephone calls, has been exacting and time-consuming. It is worth taking care at the last fence.

9
KEEP THE SHOW ON THE ROAD

No one can argue with conviction against the assertion that to offer a job in haste can lay the seeds of trouble for the future; that time must be given to every stage of recruitment and selection into management in order to reduce the risks of failure.

To busy people with an overload on their hands, this may sound all very well, but . . . .

Yes. The vacancy in a team can be a serious and expensive problem. What is more, it does tend to happen at the worst possible time. When a notice is received, the chances of a replacement being in post before the resignation takes effect are usually slim – particularly if the recommended procedures are followed. It is even worse when accident is the cause. Then there is no notice to be worked at all.

There is such a temptation to try to shorten the procedures and to cut corners. Maybe the second-best candidate has been made redundant and can start tomorrow whereas the one who so closely matches the job specification has to give three months' notice. Hard experience, however, should show that this is a trap to be avoided.

The temptation begins long before there is a choice. There are just not enough days in the week or hours in the day as it is. There is a job to be done and someone has to be found quickly. On top of that, it is being suggested here that you have to sit down and prepare a job specification; decide on a recruitment plan; spend hours on the telephone and more hours in interviewing; have people out to dinner. Really! Let's get on with it.

74

The 'temporary' solution

It may make good sense to relax and postpone all thought of making a permanent appointment for the time being. The first thing to do is to keep the show on the road and, above all, keep the customers happy.

There is an enormous pool of very competent senior executives who have retired early and who are keen to offer their services and experience on a temporary basis. They are happy to take on long or short assignments as required. There are also several agencies ready to produce them at short notice. One of these – probably the first in the field – is Executive Stand-By Ltd whose founders, John Angelbeck and Phillip Gibbs, have themselves considerable experience of consulting assignments.

At one time, there may have been fears that those on ESB's books would have come from the world of the big corporation and could not be happy in the 'nitty-gritty' atmosphere of the firm without a personnel department to take the strain of recruitment into management or where, perhaps, the demarcation line between departments was blurred. There have, in fact, been few, if any, complaints on this score. In any case, the risk of incompatibility is reduced when a contract can be terminated abruptly and without any embarrassment.

Age gap

In Chapter 2 reference was made to possible incompatibility arising from an age gap between a young employer and an employee old enough to be the parent. There is, however, no need for concern about this. The temporary nature of an assignment avoids trouble.

It can be that older people on short-term contracts will offer comment or advice, but it will be in a detached manner. They will know that their own future does not depend on the reaction of the boss. In engaging a 'temp' one can be sure of not having a 'yes man' around the place.

A trial run

It is not unknown for a stopgap to prove so satisfactory that a permanent appointment is offered. Why not? There has been a good trial run. If the job has been done well and there is mutual respect, why bother to go through all the selection procedure? You would never be able to offer an ordinary applicant, already in a secure job, a trial period, but this is different.

If the offer is accepted, this is ideal. The trouble is that so many of the 'temps' just do not want permanent jobs. It cannot be helped, but it can also be well worth trying.

Agencies such as ESB are helpful not only when there is a permanent vacancy, but also when a long illness is causing difficulty. This is discussed later (see page 111).

Time to think

It can often make sense to adopt a 'temporary' solution in an overload whether the problem looks permanent or not. As a result of being given (or buying) time to think, it may well be that a company will decide on a complete revision of the specification for a job or even of the entire management structure. This can happen because a fresh, albeit mature, mind has been brought to bear on the situation. The 'temp' will always allow his brains to be picked.

One hears of big companies bringing in teams of management consultants to examine their corporate structures and to make recommendations. No one in his right mind would suggest that kind of thing here, but put an experienced manager into a working situation, ask him or her to operate for a period so that practical knowledge can be gained, and some sound ideas can emerge particularly if they are encouraged. They will not be presented in fancy terms. They will be informally expressed – but remember, a 'temp' has no axe to grind.

Authority

We have already seen that a new vacancy created by expansion and growth will involve a delegation of authority for the first time. Without experience of this, there is a real danger that the wrong job specification will be drafted. When a permanent appointment goes awry, there is an unpleasant episode in the history of the firm. By using the temporary solution, there can be a trial period, not only for the incumbent but, even more important, for the firm. It will learn whether it has defined the job correctly.

For all these and other reasons, more and more firms, faced with management vacancies, postpone final action until the immediate pressures are taken care of and the show has been kept on the road. When the 'temp' has been in post for some months and the department is seen to be functioning well, it is time for a permanent solution to be sought without any sense of desperate urgency or heavy pressure. The risks of failure are also reduced by a considerable margin.

Image with customers

Others see objections – particularly when there is contact with customers. Those who object fear that customers, who have spoken on the telephone to A for a number of years, will be unhappy to find that B has taken over. Then, in a few months, it is C. What is wrong with this firm? It never seems to be able to hold on to managers.

Everyone in business knows that the customer is all-important and this, of course, is a factor to be considered. On the other hand, if there is going to be a hiatus after the departure of A and the arrival of C, what will the customer think of that?

The agency will usually charge a fee based upon the salary obtaining when a temporary appointment is made. It will normally be payable during the period of the contract which will be for a maximum period of one year. Bearing in mind the service it gives – if only of breathing space – it is not over-expensive.

How long will it take to have a nominee installed in post? Personal experience has shown that an executive can actually be at work within a few days. If there is a choice to be made from among several candidates, it might take a little longer. This, however, is seldom necessary. There is no commitment on either side beyond a short period and the first week or so will prove whether the contract can be extended.

The idea may not command itself to everyone. It may not always be appropriate, but it is suggested as worthy of consideration before any short cuts in the proper procedures of recruitment and selection are undertaken. It is easy, of course, to offer suggestions. Only the person in charge of a situation has the ultimate responsibility.

The offices of Executive Stand-By are:

Executive Stand-By Ltd, 310 Chester Road, Hartford, Northwich, Cheshire CW8 2AB; 0606 883849

Executive Stand-By (West) Ltd, Somercourt, Holmefield Road, Saltford, Bristol BS18 3EG; 02217 3118

Executive Stand-By (South) Ltd, Office 51, The London Fruit Exchange, Brushfield, London E1 6EU; 01–247 5693

10
SPENDING FOR PROFIT

This chapter attempts to demonstrate that before one decides on the salary to be offered for a new post, it is necessary to consider the full cost and what it is meant to achieve. Rather than start from the question, 'Can we afford it?', would it not be better to ask, 'What return will it produce?'

Money will be spent on a sales representative (salary, commission, car expenses etc) with a view to an increasing turnover. This is the line of reasoning to be applied in every department of a business. If no increase in profit is foreseen, why proceed to fill a vacancy in the management structure at all?

The case reported here is true except that the figures have been simplified for the purposes of illustration.

Overhead control

The company was a small one manufacturing clay products. It had a turnover of just over £1 million producing a profit before tax of £125,000. This was regarded as normal for the industry at the time. Its directors estimated that it was operating at about 80 per cent of capacity.

Fixed overheads were steady at £250,000. Variable costs seemed to be flashing warning lights. They were mainly in transport and energy. The basic raw material, of course, was in the quarry beside the works, but somehow the cost of extraction was rising. Unit wage costs were showing a similar tendency and the board decided that urgent action was needed to check what was an unhealthy trend. Including a few miscellaneous items, the variables had amounted to about £625,000 in the year before the action was initiated.

The accounts could be summarised as:

		£
Turnover		1,000,000
Fixed overheads	250,000	
Variables (62.5%)	625,000	875,000
Profit before tax		£125,000

It was the company secretary who brought the problem forward and it was he who suggested a line of action. He was due to retire in two years' time. He did not think modern cost control work was in his line. He was happy with historical accounting methods; he had an excellent record in the field of credit control; he believed he was good at issuing warnings, but the thought of getting involved in monitoring various cost centres in a modern way did not appeal at all. He suggested that there was an opportunity for the company to appoint his successor designate with an initial brief to investigate all the variable overheads so as to find a way of reversing the trends.

The aim, he thought, would be to cut unit wage costs back from 32 per cent to 30 per cent and energy and other overheads from 30.5 per cent to something nearer the 23 per cent of a few years back.

The idea of increasing selling prices had to be rejected. It would have been quite impractical in the economic climate of the time. Competition was too fierce.

Before making a decision, the board set out to establish the likely overall cost of a new appointment. Including on costs, it seemed this would be of the order of £25,000 in the first year. If, in that time, the variable overheads could be reduced by 7.5 per cent, the accounts would then look like this:

		£
Turnover		1,000,000
Fixed costs	275,000	
Variables (55%)	550,000	825,000
Profit before tax		£175,000

In other words, an expenditure of £25,000 would increase profits by £50,000. It sounded all very well in theory.

Break-even charts

Although the arithmetic looked satisfactory so far, what, the directors asked, would happen to the company's break-even point? When fixed overheads increase, it can follow that an increased activity rate is needed before profits are made at all. Two graphs were, therefore, drawn and they are reproduced as Figures 1 and 2.

Figure 1. *Break-even chart showing the position obtaining before a cost controller was appointed. Break even at £660,000 or 52.5% activity.*

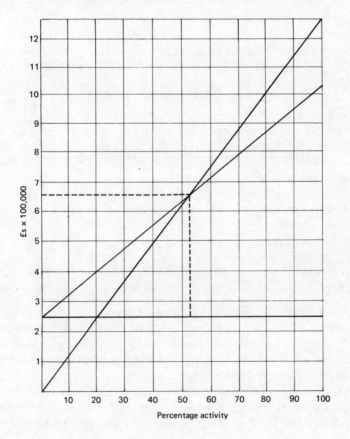

Figure 2.   *Break-even chart showing the position planned for a year after appointing a cost controller. Break even at £610,000 or 48 % activity.*

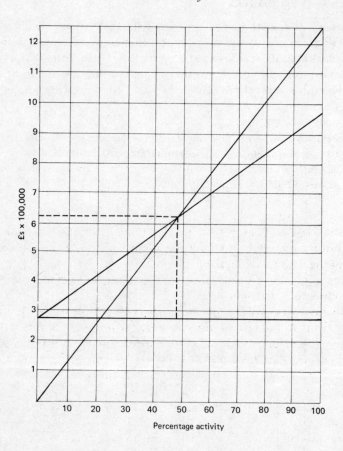

Figure 1 shows the situation as it was. Figure 2 shows the position intended after the new appointment was made. This was reassuring. The break-even point actually moved from a £660,000 turnover to £610,000. The profit potential at what was assumed to be maximum turnover had also increased.

An aim to reduce variable overheads by 7.5 per cent may sound very ambitious indeed. The board, nevertheless, decided it was possible even if it would not be achieved in the first year.

Recruitment was put in hand with a job specification for a management accountant, company secretary designate.

Six months later, a new executive took up the post and it so happened that this coincided with the half-way point in the company's financial year.

In the first full year, the target was just missed, but it was surpassed in the year after that. Not, however, without some capital investment in energy-monitoring equipment.

The anecdote illustrates how:

- a new appointment was fully assessed before recruitment was started.
- the purpose of the job could be explained fully to all candidates interviewed and there could be no possible doubt about what was expected of them.

It can be argued that no recruitment ought to have been undertaken and that with a proper management development programme, it ought to have been possible to train someone within the firm to achieve the goal.

This might have been valid if the company secretary had not been close to retirement.

Of course, it is wise to promote wherever it is possible, but not many firms of the size of our clayworks will have a number two company secretary waiting in the wings for the retirement of number one. There is often a time and place for the introduction of a new broom. In the view of this board of directors, this was one.

The story also illustrates how, when a vacancy occurs, it is not always right to seek a carbon copy of the outgoing manager. Circumstances alter over the years and companies develop. A retirement can provide an opportunity for new ideas. At least, it is a time for a fresh look at the management structure. All these and other arguments are rehearsed again in later chapters.

11
KEEPING GOOD MANAGEMENT

Having made a good appointment to the management team, you will hope the exercise is not to be repeated too often. With good people around you, you will want to keep them. Even if you have those ambitious folk whom you know are using your firm as steps in career development, you will hope that, when the time for parting comes, it will be on friendly terms. You will hope, too, for lasting goodwill based on happy years (however few) that will give you the kind of reputation you need – if only in which to find successors.

In the company where the manager is recruited and selected by the one to whom he or she will report without the intervention of a personnel manager, a great deal will depend on personal relationships. There has to be trust, confidence and, in modern parlance, communication. All these apply just as much to the thrusting and ambitious as to the plodder who lacks any initiative at all, but who suits the boss.

Career structure

Big corporations can offer job satisfaction with defined career structures within a formalised training and development programme, including long periods on courses at planned intervals. A young graduate joining the multinational organisation can expect regular reviews of progress and opportunities opening up all over the world. The only bar, it seems, to a climb to the top of the greasy pole and a knighthood or equivalent is personal ability and capacity. All this, of course, depends upon a sophisticated set-up which cannot exist in the majority of firms.

It may even be suggested by some that a young graduate joining a smaller company will be going into a kind of career cul-de-sac simply because it will not be offering all this planning.

Choosing where to live

Fortunately, not everyone wants to be in a framework lacking any degree of certainty about future location – perhaps to be required to go off at relatively short notice to spend some years in a quite unacceptable part of the globe, with consequent disregard to the wishes of the marriage partner and interruption to the children's education.

The pundits of the Confederation of British Industry and other similar bodies frequently express regret that young people are put off the idea of working in industry. Do they realise that one reason for this is the way industry is seen to push folk around? Many fathers tell their sons and daughters to avoid working for the industrial and commercial giants because they ought to be able to choose where they live. Go into a profession is so often the advice. Better to be a solicitor in a small country practice than to be a budding tycoon, never knowing where you will have to go next on your way through life.

This gives the firm without a formalised structure an advantage which it should exploit when seeking to recruit managers and even more when wanting to keep them. If you feel the need to open a new branch in another town and you believe the very person to run it is already with you, you can, at least, discuss the matter rather than make a posting.

Trust and confidence

From the start of an appointment, there has to be a strong desire for the building of trust and confidence on both sides. Where all levels of a firm are in close touch with the chief executive, there is nothing remote in the relationship. If the boss trusts the other managers, they will reciprocate. If anything happens to break this trust; if the management gets the idea it is being 'used'; if it is being called upon to take the blame which belongs elsewhere; if the boss has little regard for others; then a wound is opened which will take a long time to heal – if it ever does. It can become so bad that everyone begins to study the 'sits vac'.

Loyalty

It is useless to expect unquestioning loyalty to the firm without correlation. 'I have built this firm from nothing – it is mine' can be a perfectly natural emotion in the entrepreneur and it will usually be true. But it does not form, by itself, the foundation for loyalty from other employees – even from those who have been brought on to the board. The 'treat them mean and keep them keen' plan may have worked in the days of Gradgrind, but the world has moved on.

Once managers start leaving to seek job satisfaction and pastures where they hope their efforts will be more appreciated, the firm can become like the one described in Chapter 6 which was unable to recruit a dye house manager.

Communication

To be able to do a job properly, a manager needs to be as fully informed as possible about the business, or at least that part of it which concerns him or her.

If the firm is having a bad time, it will be fairly obvious to the alert manager. If the whole truth is withheld, it can only encourage a belief in the worst. No one with any sense would ever suggest that every least detail about the overdraft and what the bank manager is saying should be given to the shop floor, but a manager is entitled to understand the position, to know what is being done and even to be invited to offer suggestions. It is seldom clever to say, 'It is none of their/your business.' A person's future and that of his or her family are at stake.

If there is a leak or breach of confidence, the lack of loyalty is not on the part of the boss who is entitled to remonstrate. It will have revealed a misjudgement of character, but it need not upset a relationship unless it is of an outstandingly serious nature. Then it may be necessary to take drastic action and part with someone's services.

Friendship and social contact

In a big company, no one expects the chairman and his wife (or husband in the case of a female chairman) to be personal and intimate friends of the second- or third-line managers and their families. Nor is it obligatory for other managers to be close friends of the rest of the staff. Social interests are probably different anyway. Nevertheless, there is every reason for them all to know each other and be on amicable terms. A great deal can be said in favour of a firm's social gathering every year or so when all the employees' wives and husbands can get to know one another. Sometimes, this can be combined with attendance at a convention or a similar event organised by the trade association.

The main object must be to engender a feeling that all belong to a friendly set-up where there is good teamwork. The most lavish 'thrash', however, will achieve nothing if there is the wrong atmosphere at work.

The awful truth was once revealed when a small boy at a firm's family party went to the chief executive and informed him 'My daddy says you are an old skinflint.' There were no more similar parties after that and it seems the boss never took the lesson to heart. Perhaps it was also fortunate that he did not discover the small boy's name. The only comment here is that to include children in this kind of party is probably to carry things too far.

Is salary all that matters?

There is no apology for putting the question of human relations in a management structure before the more material considerations. But none of the thoughts expressed here will be of much use if, in the words of that small boy, the boss really is regarded as a skinflint. Every manager is entitled to feel that he or she is getting a just reward for what he or she is putting into the firm. It makes sense, therefore, to have regular reviews of salary and other emoluments.

In this the smaller firm or the one in which a department operates with a degree of autonomy, free of the policies designed by a personnel department, has an advantage. It can ignore the formalities and the whole picture can be discussed with each member of a team in complete confidence. This can – and should –

be done face to face and in privacy. A manager, treated with good faith like this, can understand how much he is regarded as having contributed to profits and will have a sense of belonging. If there is also a healthy bonus from the previous year's profits on top of a rise in salary, the recipient will feel even more appreciated. If there is no such thing, at least the reason can be explained and understood.

Money is important, but there are many who are attracted by more publicly visible status symbols and evidence of the regard in which they are held by the firm. Perks such as cars may be ever more harshly taxed as benefits in kind, yet it is still obvious that they give enormous satisfaction when the make or model is 'traded up'. To be seen driving a bigger and better model car than last year does a great deal for the morale of some and it improves the image among the neighbours if not also the customers.

There are other things such as health insurance which can also be very highly appreciated – particularly by the families – and pay dividends in loyalty.

Shares

When a manager is given shares in a small company, there is a feeling of being part of it. It is the first step towards the boardroom and so long as more than 50 per cent of the equity remains under control of the original owners, there is no serious dissipation. The reward in a growing commitment can be tremendous.

Such a step, however, must not be taken too soon. No one wants a shareholder in a close company to be working for a competitor. This could happen if there is a parting of the ways for any reason. Shares should go only to those managers who really give confidence that they are with the company for life and happy to be there, but the knowledge that the shares have been given will become an incentive for others.

Service agreements

Those working for the private company – whatever its size – may be afraid that they will be victims of a takeover and will become redundant at an awkward age.

In face, the private company will never have to face the kind of hostile bid which hits the headlines from time to time. A takeover, nevertheless, does happen when someone in the owning family wants to release cash. Maybe 'Aunt Jessica' has died and left her not inconsiderable holding to the wrong side of a family feud and the problem has not been foreseen as it should. Perhaps it is just that the founder of the business wants to retire and his children have other interests.

The manager who is doing a good job will feel more secure with a service agreement and it is wise to give some sort of insurance against these risks. Like shares, this is not something to be dished out too easily, but it can be far less risky and almost as satisfying to the recipient.

In seeking to retain a good team, however small, it is important that every member of it should feel part of it. The boss who sets out to provide job satisfaction will reap dividends. Failure to do so can mean an inability to attract or keep the right people. A happy firm is one for which men and women like to be known to be working.

Notwithstanding all this, the entrepreneur has to remember that the whole company is his or her child and no one else will love it as a parent. No employee will ever have such deep personal devotion to it, but the closer everyone is brought to that degree of commitment, the happier it will be.

12
SALARY, BONUS, COMMISSION AND PROFIT SHARE

In preparing a job specification (Chapter 2) one may have difficulty in fixing the salary, but before recruitment starts it is vital to pitch the total remuneration package at a level which will attract applicants of the right calibre – no more, no less. Offer too little and the quality will be poor; make it all too much and there will be a response from the over-qualified or over-experienced who will never get the job satisfaction you want to offer.

Take advice

If in doubt, the employer may do well to seek the advice of an agency before recruiting, but it is also worth doing a form of job evaluation within the firm. How does this job rate in value against other placed in the team? Is the production manager of the same, greater or less importance than, say, the company secretary? If they are thought to be equal, does a professional qualification (eg MIProdE versus FCA) carry a lot of weight? This will only work, of course, if all the salaries are fair and, what is more, up to date.

Whatever may be said here, every company will have its own peculiarities and will fix basic salaries from a mixture of common sense and 'market forces'. Any executive selection consultant can give examples of firms who have had a severe shock when someone with long service has left or retired and it has been found that the pay has just not kept pace with the outside world. It has then become necessary, perhaps, to bring in a new manager at as much as twice the salary paid hitherto.

Reviews

For this reason alone regular reviews are wise. Perhaps there is a plodder who never complains that his or her salary has been eroded by time, but this person will not be immortal. One day, too, he or she could wake up to the facts of life.

In Chapter 11, it was recommended that all management remuneration should be reviewed at regular intervals. There is, in Britain, a long tradition of the annual wage round. Maybe the system of national agreements is breaking down in favour of plant or, maybe, district or regional bargaining. This does not mean the end of the annual ritual. The smaller the company, the less likely it is that management trade unions will come into the picture. How therefore, should this review be carried out?

Quite simply, the board or the chief executive has to decide how much can be afforded. Once this figure has been reached, it can be distributed on some scale that will be regarded as fair.

Many a company thinks it is satisfactory to improve management salaries in general by the same percentage as has been agreed with the trade unions for the manual workers. Provided the team is content, this will work for a time, but the contentment is not likely to last. The method never allows for 'wage drift'. The wage earners, somehow, are almost always paid more than the figure emerging from the round because of things like overtime. Then the day arrives when a big adjustment is forced upon the company in order to bring salaries into line. Not only does this cause a big jump in costs. It has to be done in an atmosphere of dissatisfaction which could have been avoided with reasonable foresight.

It is better to avoid this situation by a system of proper reviews based on a realistic understanding of an individual's importance to the firm. Most managers can feel a sense of job satisfaction when they are offered a salary adjustment based on an appreciation of their efforts and achievements over a period of time.

Profit share

Once decided and agreed, a salary increase becomes permanent. A figure awarded after a highly successful or 'boom' year carries on through the lean times and becomes a base line for next time. For this reason if for no other, it makes good sense to look at schemes for profit-sharing. They have the advantage of entailing no commitment for the future. The disadvantage in some eyes is that they carry less of a feeling of security and can make personal domestic budgeting more difficult. Generally, therefore, most companies will regard their profit-sharing schemes as a 'top up' on reasonable basic salaries.

There are many ways of formulating profit-sharing schemes, but in most companies there seems to be one favourite way of deciding how much is available for paying out when the year's results are known.

The first call on profits will always be the business itself. This is the amount needed to be ploughed back for new investment or simply to finance growth. Many an expanding firm will find that little, if any, of a growing profit is cash in the bank. Those unfamiliar with the way things can be, find it hard to understand that a doubled turnover can mean twice the level of stocks and work in progress, twice the book debts and a big increase in the overdraft. It is a simple fact of life often ignored by the presenters of wage claims. At least managers can be asked to understand.

After a 'plough back' it is reasonable to think of the shareholders and to pay them a dividend.

The amount available for sharing out is thus calculated as profit after tax, less retention and dividend. The bottom line of this calculation will then be adjusted if the share-out will reduce the tax requirement, but this will depend on the terms of the most recent Finance Act.

A decision can now be made on the method of distribution. There is one school of thought which suggests that all managers should have a pro-rata figure based on salaries. If this provides an appreciable sum, perhaps most will be happy and regard it as fair. It will be much more difficult, but may be more equitable, to allocate it according to merit.

A more complex merit scheme may well prove necessary except in the very small firm where there is an intimacy and understanding between all members of the team.

Bonus or commission?

Except where differing levels of payment are made in a profit share, resentment may build up and there may be a feeling that personal effort by an individual manager is not being rewarded, that a 'passenger' is being 'carried'. When this happens, the profit-sharing scheme begins to defeat its own object.

Then one may be well advised to consider a bonus scheme where everyone will know from the start of the year how personal earnings will be calculated and that they will be the result of personal achievement or effort.

A simple illustration of a bonus scheme can be given by reference to sales commission. This is usually a flat percentage of turnover, but this does not set targets with real incentive to reach them. In Chapter 2 it was recorded that a management consultant needs to generate fee levels of four times salary before breaking even. This factor may be high and the break-even point of the average may not be so simple to calculate for every management discipline. It can, however, make sense to try to estimate one if possible. It can then be decided at which point a commission or bonus should start to be paid. Once this is fixed, there can be a graduation of rate as sales increase. Rather than pay a basic salary plus x per cent on all sales, something like the following formula can emerge which will enable profits on increased turnover to be shared with the individual:

Sales £	Commission per cent
0– 20,000	nil
20,001 – 25,000	1
25,001 – 30,000	2
30,001 – 35,000	3
35,001 – 40,000	4
40,001 – 50,000	6
50,001 – 75,000	8
75,000 upwards	10

These figures are, of course, completely hypothetical and will bear no relation to reality in any company. They are meant only to illustrate a principle. Many firms do, however, operate schemes of this kind and they seem to work well. The individual is able to see clearly when a profit is emerging from his efforts and how it is passed on or shared out.

Obviously, a scale like this must be reviewed annually to take account of changes in basic salary, adjustment of selling prices etc. The starting point for a bonus will also have to move in relation to the cost of keeping the individual in post – the personal break-even.

The example for a sales executive is given because it is simple to illustrate. With thought, it can be adapted to all departments in a business. The production manager, for instance, is responsible for the firm's total output. Why not a scale based on invoices issued? Might not the purchasing manager or buyer be given a scale based on the raw material content of turnover?

If payments can be progressive from the beginning of the year, there will be an increasing bonus each month. This is usually found to give the greatest incentive to effort but, if it places too big a burden on the accounts department, the calculations can be made quarterly, half yearly or even yearly. The longer periods are, however, not recommended. There is a great deal to be said in favour of a constantly increasing pay packet as the year advances.

Whatever method of incentive payment is devised, it is essential that it is not only fair, but is seen to be fair by all. It must also be beyond argument that the target figures are more than attainable. No one likes pie in the sky.

It used to be said about one company that it had a first-class pension scheme. No one knew what it was because no one ever stayed long enough to find out. They all left because the salaries and commission rates were not fair. No one could earn what had been indicated as possible.

13
WHAT ABOUT TRAINING?

The company secretary described in Chapter 10 was near to retirement. Even so, some would argue with justice that the solution adopted was just too easy. Suppose he had been ten years younger; would the board have been forced either to teach an old dog new tricks or face the human problem of redundancy?

To have 'let him go', apart from what it would have done to a loyal servant of the company in his fifties and, moreover, to his family, could have had serious repercussions throughout the company. 'The way they treated old George after all his years in the firm . . .' could conjure up the thought, 'Will it happen to me?'

It will be recalled that it was the company secretary himself who had seen the need for a new skill. Whether he ought to have recognised it sooner or whether, indeed, the directors were really as alert as they should have been are good questions which cannot be answered here. Might it have been that the proper action lay in the field of management training or even in a quite different department of the firm? Was it, indeed, an accountancy matter at all?

Training associations

Throughout the country, there are training associations in which smaller companies have come together to provide training facilities (on and off the job) for their employees. They usually work closely with the local technical colleges.

It is in this sort of context, alas, that industrial training is seen as a way of producing competent operatives rather than one of developing and fostering good management and spreading knowledge of modern methods. Yet there have been remarkable changes in techniques. Whole new attitudes are needed in the firm which hopes to stay in the race.

Can one imagine the small firm of solicitors or accountants where the partners, once qualified, fail to keep abreast of changes in the law? Yet so many of our industrial and commercial companies seem not to recognise the necessity of keeping their managers (including, let it be said, the chief executives) up to date. There is all too often a tendency to modernise only when there is a retirement or someone leaves. A new executive arrives with new ideas and they are adopted. Then that department ossifies for a couple of decades until there is another succession.

Watch for deficiencies

It is always profitable to ensure that people are encouraged to update their skills, to look for opportunities for increasing efficiency. Where the top management is, itself, ever on the watch for indications of room for improvement, it will usually find a ready response at second and third line. It can never be right, anyway, to wait until there is an urgent problem. Far better to look ahead and plan for future needs.

When that urgent problem is staring the company in the face, it can mean that recruitment is essential. The only alternative may be that a member of a small team who can ill be spared must go off on a crash course. Either way, the solution will take some time to be reached.

Who to train and how?

By looking ahead and recognising a need before it is pressing, it is possible to decide with proper consideration who should be trained and how. At the risk of tedium, let us go back to our company secretary friend. Suppose he had been ten years younger or the warning signs had been seen much sooner. Was it not possible that a more vigilant managing director could have arranged a form of training which, indeed, might not have involved the company secretary at all? Is it not conceivable that responsibility for cost control might have been better laid at the door of the production management? Would it have been better to have sent someone from there on a course than to have produced, in effect, a new job specification in the administration?

From fitter to sales manager

Some years ago, a young electrical fitter in a small firm was involved in a very serious motor accident to the point where he was unable to stand at his bench. It was thought he would be in that position for some months though fit in every other way.

It also happened that, just at the time he came out of hospital, the firm's estimator left for another job.

As a stop gap in order to help the fitter, the managing director offered him the chance of the sedentary position until he was completely recovered. There was no doubt the young man had the required knowledge of the company and its products. To that extent, he would have a head start over any newly recruited estimator, but there was nevertheless a doubt (on both sides) about the chances of a really satisfactory move from a manual to a clerical occupation. Could a skilled fitter become a pen pusher?

Remarkably, the experiment was an outstanding success. The technical background was there to enable the estimating work to be done with accuracy. Customers who spoke to the new voice on the telephone had a high opinion of his competence and manner and this soon filtered back to the boss. The man himself expressed surprise that what he had expected to be a boring job was full of interest. A permanent appointment followed. What is more, the subject of what had been regarded as a risky experiment accepted that there was a need for personal development. After two training courses (one by correspondence) he became the company's sales manager when the department was created. The sales representatives respected him too. Even if he had never been 'on the road' he showed he knew the principles of sales management and his product knowledge was superb.

From typist to sales rep

A company in the north had a London office. The London staff consisted of a sales executive and a woman who was his secretary. Her job was to act as a liaison between customers and the works. She had come to the firm with little more than a secretarial (ie shorthand and typing) qualification, but over some five years she gained considerable knowledge of the products and what the customers in the south wanted. When the executive was approaching retirement, the managing director began to look at the succession problem. Why not, he thought, offer the secretary the chance of going into the field? She took fright at the idea but, after some persuasion, she agreed, as she put it, to dip her toe in the water to test the temperature.

She found the work interesting, but asked for some sales training. This was provided and the result was a success. Customers to whom she had spoken welcomed her when she called and she turned out to be the best rep the company had ever had.

Look within

The moral of these two stories is that it can often pay good dividends to look for management within the firm. Was there an operative in the Chapter 10 company who, with training, could have become a cost controller? After all, he would start with a far better product knowledge than a new recruit.

Maybe it is not always easy to spot a potential manager on the shop floor, but when it happens successfully, it does wonders for morale and creates a feeling of appreciation. This is one of the best ways of retaining management. There are many firms (both small and large) which began as one or two man/woman operations. The first employee may have been, say, a machine operator who worked with the founder of the business to the point of becoming a colleague. A mutual trust then developed and two people became, in effect, the management as others joined the payroll. Once growth is there, of course, it becomes more difficult to be confident about translating from shop floor to management. It can seldom be done without recourse to some form of training.

Sales representatives do not always make good sales managers by simply being taken 'off the road'. They do, however, have the product knowledge and the customer contact and with guidance in management principles and techniques may well be able to develop the basic qualities and do far better than someone brought in over their heads.

Too busy to learn?

Partly because of the present-day political overtones attaching to training, some managing directors believe that the whole subject smacks of bureaucracy and formality. They have been heard to say it is all very well to let apprentices have day release and the like, but the management is (or ought to be) far too busy to think of going on courses. This is unfortunate, to say the least. All that is needed is a constant and regular review of the skill situation so that everyone is motivated towards personal development. If suggestions are welcome in the boardroom and they are always given fair consideration, they will come forward.

It will always be nonsense to try to lay down strict guidelines to cover every single enterprise in every field of industry and commerce. Each firm has its own personality.

It used to be fashionable to deride the managing director who would insist that his was a peculiar industry or that his firm was not like others. Both these remarks were made almost every day to management consultants. The wise ones recognised the truth. Every firm in every industry *is* different from all the others.

Define objectives

This does not mean that a firm ought to find it impossible to define its objectives adequately and to the point where training can be arranged to close any gaps which are likely to open up later. If there is a wish to see the firm grow, there ought to be some kind of plan which will enable it to retain good managers by helping them to develop to their own satisfaction and to the mutual welfare of both them and the company.

There is much to be said in favour of a regular (perhaps annual or bi-annual) face-to-face discussion with senior managers on this subject. This should make it possible to recognise the need for new skills before they are urgent. When they are identified, thought can be given to possible candidates for training within the firm so as to promote rather than recruit.

Imagine the situation where the managing director goes to ask the bank manager for an increased overdraft and he is asked for a sight of the business plan. Neither the managing director nor the company secretary has even heard of the term, let alone knows how to compile one. Perhaps the auditor would be able to help, but would it not be so much better for the question to have been anticipated and for the plan to have been on paper before the bank manager had been approached? At least the overdraft would have been more likely to have been allowed. This is not such a stupid example as it might seem. Ask any bank manager.

Self-assessment

If all managers are encouraged to raise the question of training with the boss, a system of self-assessment will emerge of its own volition. Individuals will draw attention to their own training needs with a confidence that they will not be selling themselves short. No one will be afraid of exposing personal weaknesses.

In times of recession, when every effort is being made to cut overheads, there is always a temptation to reduce or even eliminate expenditure on training. This is understandable and it can be prudent to postpone long-term plans, but it must be right to keep up the efficiency of the company in some directions. If, by attending a one- or two-day seminar, someone can come back with an idea which will bring in more business or cut a cost, why refuse to let it happen?

Training can be used to eliminate the need for recruitment by a reappraisal of existing practices. A knowledge of a firm, its practices, its customers and its products or services will always give a promoted existing employee a head start over a new person, but it will do more. A good chief is always wise to consider the effect a new broom will have. There can be resentment by those who think they ought to have been shown preferment.

There may also be a case to be argued the other way. There may be relief that, at last, a deficiency has been noticed and that steps have been taken to fill a gap. It is essential to beware of a danger that a firm is growing stale and, not having brought in any new blood for a long time, is becoming in-bred and introspective. There will always be some jobs which can be filled only by someone with a particular professional qualification. If there is only one person with it in the company, and that person leaves or dies, recruitment is the only course.

Group discussion

A very effective method of management training is the group discussion. It can take place in the formal atmosphere of the boardroom in working hours and be led by a professional instructor retained for the occasion; or it can simply be a brainstorming session in a private room of a pub. In this kind of training the boss can and probably should play a part.

Trade associations

Valuable lessons can be gleaned from meetings organised by trade associations and employers' organisations. Those which organise a relatively short formal agenda, with plenty of time for circulation over coffee and a buffet lunch, provide for a dissemination of ideas. There is no question, of course, of an exchange of commercially sensitive information between competitors, but one will learn enough of what is going on in an industry to indicate there may be skill problems ahead at home.

The trade association is also well equipped to arrange for seminars on subjects of peculiar concern to an industry. It will often join in lobbying activities with other organisations whose members have similar problems. Apart from their political lobbying, the trade associations can organise seminars and other events which will help member firms to deal with mutual management problems. Think of the way in which the energy-intensive industries have helped by running training sessions for companies needing to achieve economies in fuel consumption at a time of steeply rising prices.

Danger of over-training

Having said all this, it has to be recognised that there can be dangers in over-training. Encourage folk to acquire knowledge and skill they cannot use and there is frustration. It can lead to a search for somewhere else to use the training acquired at your expense. Then, far from helping to keep good management, it becomes counterproductive.

Sources of training

Once a need is established, it will be found that there is no shortage of advice as to where the necessary courses are available. Some sources are listed in Appendix E but, once again, the industry's trade association will always be a good starting point. Maybe it will not know the answer to a question, but it will know someone who does. So will the Department of Employment.

There is an old saying that the best form of training is to be had at the school of experience. There is no denying this, but it is not always possible to gain relevant experience in new techniques within the company confines. The introduction of computer accounting; an innovation like robotics; the need for fluency in a foreign language in the sales department: all these and other examples spring to mind as instances where someone will almost certainly have to go outside the firm to be trained.

Should the top manager of all – the boss – be prepared to submit to training? Perhaps it will be essential and almost certainly wise. This book is about finding good managers. It could be argued that the proprietor is unlikely to leave anyway, but could it be that the boss who shows willingness to learn will command more respect? The answer will probably differ from one firm to the next, but there is no harm in asking the question.

British industry and commerce is often compared badly with that of the USA, Germany and, above all, Japan, for neglect of training. One reads constant reports of shortages of skilled operatives at times and in areas of high unemployment. It is just as important to think of training managers as it is of producing skilled operatives. It could even be that, with more attention to the management field, some of the shortages on the shop floor could be eliminated by better organisation.

14
DISCRIMINATION

The Race Relations Act and the Sex Discrimination Act are almost carbon copies of each other. Their provisions extend from recruitment via terms and conditions of employment to access to training schemes, benefits and opportunities for promotion. There is 'direct' discrimination and 'indirect'. One can be accused of discriminating even if what one has done has never resulted in an actual case. For instance, if one advertises for a person with an A level pass in a subject, it may be held to prevent an overseas student from applying if the country of origin does not have A level examinations. One should ask for A level or similar.

An employer can be held liable for discrimination by an employee. It is no defence to say you did not know. It is necessary to show that all reasonable and practicable steps have been taken to prevent discrimination.

Danger at recruitment and selection

A potential employer is in the greatest danger of falling foul of these laws during the period of recruitment and selection.

The first and most valuable safeguard lies in the carefully and properly prepared job specification. If it sets out all the requirements – particularly experience, qualifications and mobility – it will be a valuable shield throughout the entire exercise.

Advertising copy
From the specification, advertising copy can be drafted in a way which will avoid initial problems. Indeed, here is a good argument

103

for using the experience of an advertising agent with a classified department. The good copy writer will know the pitfalls and how to avoid them.

Selecting for interview

In deciding who to interview, there can be careful comparison of personal details with the requirement and notes can be made showing where there are deficiencies. Then, if one is called upon, it will be possible to demonstrate clearly why a person was rejected – not because of sex or colour, but because of failure to meet the needs as well as others.

Prepare questions

In interviews, it must also be clear beyond any doubt that no one was asked questions not also posed to others and which could be interpreted as racist or sexist.

Both the Equal Opportunities Commission and the Commission for Racial Equality have issued literature describing leading or typical cases before tribunals. One leaflet from the EOC describes a claim by a woman because the following questions were put to her by an interviewing panel:

- What was her relationship to her husband?
- Was she Mrs or Miss?
- Was she legally separated from her husband?
- Did she intend to have a family in the near future?

It was held that these questions were discriminatory because similar questions were not put to other (male) applicants. The leaflet does not record how she knew.

No need for offence

On reflection, it becomes obvious that there was no need at all for offence to be given – even if the woman concerned showed herself to be extremely militant. Her paper qualifications must have shown her to be as worthy of consideration as the men. They ought to have been the basis of all the questions put to her and to the others as well.

One wonders whether the panel concerned had studied the job requirements in detail or even whether these had been adequately defined in the first place. If the whole series of interviews had been properly planned and all questions to candidates thought out, it would have made sense for all candidates (men and women) to have been asked something like:

- Does your spouse have any commitments or a job which might make you less mobile than our job specification requires?
- Do the working hours requirements create any problems or difficulties for you or your family?
- Do you and your spouse use the same surname in your working life?
  (Why this matters is a good question, but it gets round the Miss, Mrs or Ms point.)
- Is there any possibility that family problems will occur with regard to your children's schools or examinations?

Having posed questions like that, one is surely free to put supplementaries arising from the answers and to do so without risk. It would, for instance, become apparent if husband and wife were separated or if a woman was Mrs or Miss – even if the relevance of the point remains obscure.

Even in the smallest firms, there are too many cases brought before tribunals where a candidate feels aggrieved and jumps to the conclusion that the real reason for failure to get a job is either sex or race. These hearings are, at best, time-consuming and, at worst, expensive. The firm which presents a well-prepared job specification, and can show how carefully only the best qualified people have been called to interview and that they have then been assessed on an equal basis, has little to worry about.

Less discrimination now

When militant racism and feminism cases hit the headlines, they are often counterproductive and make many prospective employers wary of even considering very worthy candidates. However, there is also a growing realisation that human resources are dwindling with a falling birth rate. In 1981, there were 900,000 boys and girls of 18 years of age in Britain. By 1995, that figure will have dipped to 600,000. With such a trend, there can only be increasing competition for the talent and services of both sexes.

In any case, intelligent women today want not only jobs, but properly structured careers.

When one looks at the statistics for school-leavers over, say, the past 20 years one sees an increasing entry by girls into A levels. University figures also show the same trend. What is more, the percentage pass rates seem always to be greater among girls than boys. Maybe girls take courses because they want to, while boys enter because they think they ought to.

After starting off in a career, many girls drop out of the race in favour of the traditional family role. Some find it hard to get back later when they wish, but they will nearly all have retained a basic management ability. It is here that the company which has (or needs) no strict personnel policies ought to recognise the opportunities to attract by offering induction courses.

In Chapter 11 it was argued that there were attractions in the company unlikely to move managers around at short notice. This kind of firm must surely be the kind to appeal to the married woman.

Try positive discrimination

Might not all this point towards an argument in favour of the operation of one of the provisions of the Discrimination Acts? It is lawful to take positive action to recruit a woman into a predominantly male management structure. The law states that where there have been few or no members of one sex in particular work in a company for the previous 12 months, an employer is allowed to give special encouragement to the minority sex.

Demographers are making all kinds of predictions about population trends and what they may mean to industry or commerce in the generations yet to come. The director, partner or proprietor of the smaller company or the senior manager recruiting free of hidebound personnel policies wants only to find and keep the best possible talent in the team. This means it must be time to think of using the discrimination laws to advantage and actually draw up a job specification or two so as to attract women candidates.

In earlier chapters, stress was laid on the need for compatibility among those working together in management. If a man finds he has a candidate before him whose face, quite bluntly, is not going to fit, there can be problems when, also, that person is black, female or, perhaps worst of all, both. There are always dangers that 'body language' or even a chance remark will be taken the wrong way. Then simple and sheer cussedness can bring a reference to a tribunal. It can only be avoided by vigilance and care. No decent individual will deliberately set out to be offensive. All one can do is to be on one's guard throughout the whole of a selection procedure. So long as the interview is conducted on planned lines and all questions are put with strict relevance and reference to the job specification, one has a defence.

When all is said and done, any prospective employer must have the right to choose who will fill any vacancy. If it can be shown beyond peradventure that every candidate has been given a fair chance and that qualifications and experience have been checked meticulously against the requirements, no claim in respect of discrimination will succeed. It must also be reasonable to say, 'In my judgement X was the most suitable applicant.'

15
RETAIN OR FIRE?

One can take every possible precaution aimed at reducing the risks of failure in recruiting and selecting management. In spite of this, whatever one does, however one does it, however hard one tries, the risks are always there. One is dealing with human beings. It can, therefore, be necessary to face up to an uncomfortable and unpleasant dilemma when the man or woman selected for a job turns out to lack some essential characteristic or quality. It means, simply, that there is a square peg in a round hole. What is to be done?

Gradgrind, of course, would have had no compunction. He would have shown the door immediately. Nor, it seems, does it matter so much in some of our big corporations where the top manager is protected by the intervention of the sophisticated personnel department. The square peg can be moved to another hole elsewhere in the organisation. But times have changed for the majority of industry and commerce. Every time a manager is relieved of his post (except, perhaps, in a case of gross misconduct) there is a ripple of unease throughout the organisation. The smaller the firm, the greater the need for a bond of mutual trust among all the management team. Unless everyone is pulling the same way, progress is bound to be inhibited and may well be replaced by regression.

The reputation of the 'hirer and firer' soon spreads to affect the company in other ways. It can acquire a reputation which will make good people afraid to work in it. It can even harm relations with customers.

The managing director who appoints someone and then sacks the same person a few months later can come to be regarded as lacking in judgement and this can lead to a loss of respect for other decisions.

Whose fault?

The sensible employer also recognises that the selection process is a two-sided affair. Who offered the job, and therefore, whose fault is it that things have gone wrong?

Paragons, of course, are few and far between. The candidate who was offered the job must have had some qualities that appealed. Can they not still be harnessed and the situation saved by a look at that original job specification? Maybe this is a vain hope, but it is surely worth more than a passing thought. One can hope that, with a mutually agreed amendment avoiding any form of constructive dismissal, the situation can be saved.

Long service

It is far more difficult when a manager with long service proves not to be up to the job as it has evolved. Perhaps some new, modern process has been put into operation or is needed and it is beyond his or her capability. Maybe ill health is causing long absences. Perhaps the firm has grown and it has become obvious that there is a total inability to cope or to delegate and a whole department is being neglected with a knock-on effect throughout the firm.

Whatever the cause, whatever the background, it is essential to face up to the dilemma. It is surprising how many chief executives simply funk their responsibilities in these circumstances. They postpone the evil day, hoping against hope that the problem will resolve itself. It never will. It can only get worse unless it is tackled. In a large department or organisation, maybe it is possible, though hardly wise, to carry a passenger while others provide 'cover'. In other places, this is almost certainly out of the question and neglect leads to serious trouble very soon.

The prosperity of the firm matters

Whatever action is taken, the paramount consideration must be the welfare and prosperity of the firm and everyone in it. The decision, moreover, rests where the buck always does – with the boss. Major surgery, dismissal, may in the end be unavoidable, but it should always be the last resort, particularly when one is dealing with a long-time server.

What is the reason?

A mistake in selection is most likely to be discovered within six months and, therefore, will not involve the legal requirements of fair and unfair dismissal. Otherwise an unsuitability problem will probably arise because:

- a job has grown too big for an incumbent who cannot delegate
- ill health has brought a loss of efficiency with long and frequent absences
- some major disagreement with others has grown up
- there is a need for the introduction of new methods
- the job itself has become redundant.

With any of these, there is a virtue in perfectly frank discussion with the individual concerned. From this a constructive suggestion may emerge and solve the problem. After that, it can be good practice to look at the whole management structure and to consider whether any deficiency can be taken up by another individual. It will always be important in the interests of good relations for all to see that a genuine attempt is being made to find the best answer. It is even possible that another manager will come up with a suggestion for a reorganisation. One is saying, in effect:

- Here is a problem.
- These are our resources. How can we use them so that the problem is solved?
- If we lack resources, how do we best fill the gap(s)?

Even if nothing of value emerges from this, one has, at least, shown a determination to protect the interests of the firm which provides the livelihood of those who have been consulted. This process must never look like buck-passing.

New professional qualification needed?

Suppose it is decided that a new professional qualification is needed. Then the costing exercise described in Chapter 10 will be necessary. It should also be remembered that someone with certificated professional talents will not necessarily get job satisfaction from routine and mundane tasks. Perhaps that long-serving manager whose whole life has been in the firm and is used to the old ways will still be needed after all. There could be dangers in losing the benefit of that knowledge and experience of the firm. Maybe there will be a lack of ability in the new techniques, but . . ..

Absence through illness

When problems arise because of frequent or extended illness, the firm has what is probably the most difficult of human problems. Long drawn out gaps in management in a tightly run organisation bring neglect which is felt everywhere. Worst of all, the threat of the loss of a job usually exacerbates the difficulty since anxiety will tend to impede recovery – it can even, in some cases, be fatal. There is also a sincere feeling of sympathy among colleagues which the wise employer will respect. There is a sensation of almost divided loyalty – that to the firm and that to a valued member of the staff.

Now, there is no doubt at all that a chat with the whole management team makes for good relations. All will want to do the best they can to help a colleague, but they will also see the need to think of the company and their own interests.

Assuming medical advice is that the illness is likely to be protracted and that the job cannot be 'carried' by others, the obvious short-term answer is to invoke the 'temporary' solution suggested in Chapter 9. How long this can continue will depend on what the firm can afford, but the invalid may well feel content to forgo at least part of his or her sick pay if he or she is assured of a secure return to the job in the end. A sense of security can aid recovery better than any medicine.

If, finally, there is little or no hope of a full and fit return to work, it may be necessary to part company. Obviously, this will be done on the best terms the company can afford. Once again, however, it will be wise to do nothing without consulting the medical practitioner involved.

A talk with the doctor dealing with a patient can prove very helpful, but can be difficult to achieve. The patient's consent is essential. Not so long ago, a managing director had decided that a departmental manager was simply not up to his job. Although the manager had been with the company a long time, there was no alternative to finding as painless a way as possible of 'letting him go'. Then the manager was taken ill. The nature of the illness was not known, but it sounded from telephone calls as if it was going to be a long one.

The managing director felt he was on the horns of a dilemma. There was no doubt at all that the man had to go, but to make the 'chop' in these circumstances and at this particular time did seem to be out of the question on grounds of humanity. What was to be done? It seemed to be sensible to have a word with the doctor and tell him what was in mind.

This brought a quite remarkable and unexpected revelation. The invalid had not felt up to his job for some considerable time and was hoping he would be declared redundant. Far from being inhuman to give him the sack, it would be a kindness – even an act of mercy.

The best possible redundancy terms were arranged and, believe it or not, recovery was speeded. This was a turn-up for the book. When he decided to talk to the doctor, the managing director had not had the slightest indication that the solution would be so simple.

It is unlikely that this experience will be repeated very often in a lifetime, but it does indicate that things may not always be as they seem and a word with an invalid's doctor can lead to a fresh line of thought.

The last resort – dismissal

Having tried, and having been seen to have tried, to find every possible alternative to dismissal, it may be that, in the end, there is no alternative. That man or woman must go. It is now that the legal position has to be considered. Once appointed to a job, a manager has exactly the same rights under the law as the most junior employee. Every firm has to realise that a reference to a tribunal on grounds of unfair dismissal is not only time-consuming and, possibly, expensive; it can also harm the firm's reputation as an employer.

Every dismissed employee who has been with a company for more than six months is entitled to demand a written statement giving the reasons; after a year's service (two years in firms employing 20 or less) the statement may be used in evidence at a tribunal when unfair dismissal is claimed.

To be fair, dismissal must be because of:

- lack of capability or qualification on the part of the employee to do the job for which he or she was engaged (this can include health)
- misconduct
- redundancy
- some new law which makes the job impossible of fulfilment
- some other substantial reason justifying dismissal such as personality conflict, business reorganisation etc.

At first sight, one might think that these definitions would enable a harsh employer to give the sack almost with impunity. Look again. 'Capability' can be a subjective term and note that bit about 'on the part of the employee to do the job for which he or she was engaged'. 'Personality conflict' may sound very wide-ranging, but if someone has been with a firm for more than a couple of years, and there is this problem, whose fault is it? It takes two to make a quarrel.

Any employer facing up to the need for dismissal on any grounds at all will always be wise to seek the professional advice of his trade association or, failing that, the local office of the Advisory Conciliation and Arbitration Service (ACAS). There is no shortage of literature on the subject. It is all worth reading, but there is no substitute for the comment and guidance of someone with expertise and, above all, a detached view.

One thing needs to be emphasised. If the proposed dismissal is on the grounds of conduct (other than gross misconduct), lack of capability or ill health, it should not be sudden. A tribunal will expect to find that there has been a procedure based upon natural justice as well as legal principle. It will always be recommended that this be in three stages:

1. An informal warning.
2. A formal warning in writing referring to the earlier verbal one. This should set out the nature of the complaint and also make clear what is in mind if there is no improvement.
3. A final formal warning in writing setting a time limit and making clear that dismissal will follow any failure to improve.

The period which may elapse between each of these stages can only be decided in the light of the circumstances and the nature of the complaint. Here is a good argument in favour of seeking advice from an expert sooner rather than later.

More is written in the next chapter about some of the legal pitfalls in the field of employing people, but it will all underline the need for care at every stage of recruitment and selection and every possible action to avoid the painful (and maybe expensive) consequences of mistakes arising from inadequate procedures.

16
LEGAL OBLIGATIONS

In its wisdom (some would say lack of it) Parliament has passed numerous laws on the subject of employment and employee relations. Speak to MPs of any political party during the passage of this kind of legislation and one almost always finds that they are thinking of the very big battalions and headline grabbing strikes of unhappy memory. When one refers to one's own experiences, one gets the reaction, 'Oh, yes. But this bill is not meant to apply to *that* sort of situation.'

But it always does. These measures have just as much force in the medium- and smaller-sized businesses where there are no personnel managers to keep abreast and where the directors, partners and proprietors will, with justice, claim that they have more important things to do than worry about what might constitute, say, constructive dismissal or positive discrimination.

Originally, British firms with less than five employees were exempt from the laws about discrimination. The European Court decided otherwise and Parliament had to fall in line. There is no exemption now.

What is more, managers – even the top tycoons – are employees in the legal sense in the same way as the most lowly paid workers and they have the same rights. One might expect senior people to be reasonable and carry on quite well without reference to the law. Most do so, but there is always the exception to the rule who can and will catch a firm unawares at the worst possible time.

Visits from bureaucrats asking awkward questions and then bringing prosecutions will be rare. Most firms will carry on happily unaware, perhaps, of their transgressions. In the same way, few will have their premises gutted by fire but, surely, all will insure against such a disaster. In the same way they should take all precautions in the employment field. It is when some calamity occurs, such as a serious accident, that the awkward questions come to be asked.

In a case about employers' liability contested by the insurance company, the managing director can be put on the spot by an astute barrister if it is impossible to produce written particulars relating to the job in question or to the firm's rules in general. One has only to think of the fire at King's Cross tube station and what happened to top management after the public enquiry to see the point of this.

In Chapters 14 and 15, we looked at the law on discrimination and some of the rights of employees in relation to dismissal. One is of most import during recruitment and selection; the other when termination is involved. In the interests of harmony and not merely to satisfy the bureaucrat, it makes sense to get off on the right foot and stay that way.

Written contract of employment

As soon as a job has been offered and accepted, there is a contract of service. It need not be in writing to be legally binding. The terms may be simply those given verbally at an interview, but one can see immediately how dangerous it is to rely on that sort of thing. In any case an employer is required by law to give every employee written details of the main terms and conditions of employment within 13 weeks of joining the company.

Just imagine the possible risks arising from a delay to the end of that statutory period. The new manager accepts the offer of a job and then gives three months' notice to the existing employer. It could be six or even seven months before the written statement has, by law, to be provided. Memory can play tricks in an interval of that length.

If ever there was an argument for the full, carefully prepared and agreed job specification, here it is. Not only is this document a matter of common sense and sound management principle, it is a legal necessity. So produce it at the start.

The company handbook

The job specification, followed by a letter of appointment, will cover almost all the requirements of the law relating to 'written particulars', but not quite. There will be a number of general conditions in respect of work within the company which will apply to all employees. These are best set out in what is usually known as the company handbook and will include such things as:

- health and safety procedures
- grievance and discipline rules
- communication, consultation and participation
- work and works organisation
- amenities – medical, canteen etc.

A fuller description of the purpose and format of this book is contained in ACAS booklet number 9 (see Appendix D). It is not peculiar to management and it does not make sense to go into detail here. All that needs to be said is that if such a book exists, it will be a complete back-up to every job specification and with the two documents all legal requirements of 'written particulars' will have been met. The handbook need not (should not) be complicated. Nor need it be printed. A couple of photocopies of typescript will be all that is required, provided everyone knows where they can be seen. Nor need its preparation be a great burden. Most employers' organisations will be happy to help and so will ACAS. Reference to ACAS Code of Practice on Disciplinary Practice and Procedures in Employment will also be useful.

Time off and other rights

Any employee – including management – is entitled to time off from work for certain public duties such as duties as a magistrate, service on a local authority, tribunals, boards of governors of schools and colleges etc. This is unpaid and the time allowed has to be 'reasonable'. As always, this word is loosely defined and it can lead to trouble if there is not a complete understanding. As soon as a member of the management team is appointed or elected to one of these organisations, it is wise to discuss the matter and to have it in writing. In the case of a new employee, the issue should be dealt with in the contract of employment and after discussion at interview in relation to the job specification. It is all too easy for the firm to feel quite happy that it has a member of a local authority on its books, but when the demands of a particular committee grow, the gloss may wear off a little. It is then that the written agreement as to how much time can be given to the job is useful in clearing the air.

There are several other statutory rights given by law to individuals. Most depend on a qualifying period of employment. They are unlikely to have frequent impact in management and are not dealt with at length here. The following list of some, however, may be of use:

Right	Qualifying Service
Medical suspension	1 month
Guarantee pay	1 month
Trade union membership	none
Maternity pay	2 years
Maternity leave	2 years
Redundancy	2 years

Should any of the above rights appear to be relevant in a management situation, reference to the employers' organisation or to ACAS will provide all the advice needed. There may, of course, be no harm in looking at them before a job is offered if they seem relevant. They can then be covered in the job specification or the letter of appointment. On the other hand, the company handbook ought to include a statement of all employee statutory rights.

Good relations

Attention to legal requirements of employment is not only a matter of self-preservation against the day when trouble arises. It can do a great deal to promote harmony among the management. After all, the demands of the law in the present day are no more than a formulation of what good employers have been doing for a very long time. The paperwork set out above is a very strong tool in the task of keeping good managers, so long, of course, as it does not dominate the scene.

The rule, surely, should be:

Get the paperwork behind us
Know where we all stand
Then get on with the job.

APPENDICES

Appendix A
Checklist
for
Preparation of a Job Specification

1. What is the title of the job (eg works manager, office manager)?
2. What authority will be delegated?
   Personnel (hire/fire)? Limits? Overtime? Purchasing? Limits?
   Capital expenditure? Limits?
3. To whom will the person appointed be responsible?
4. For whom will he or she be responsible?
5. What are the responsibilities of the job in detail? Is any initiative to be allowed from the start?
6. What are the duties in detail?
   Principal duties
   Secondary duties.
7. What knowledge and experience are required?
   Essential
   Desirable.
8. What minimum educational level is necessary?
   Secondary (ie GCSE O and A level or similar)?
   Academic (degree etc)?
9. What technical and/or professional qualifications are required?
   Minimum essential (eg OND etc)
   Desirable or maximum (eg MIProdE etc).
10. With whom will liaison within the firm be necessary? Will this demand any special characteristic?
11. Are there any people outside the firm with whom he or she will have to deal?

Suppliers
Subcontractors
Customers.
Will any of these people demand any special qualities? What sort of things will be involved?

12. Personal details:
    Any age limits? If so, why?
    Any other relevant points?

13. Mobility required – travel:
    At home
    Abroad
    What periods of absence from home are possible or probable?

14. Conditions of service:
    Period of notice on either side
    Any service agreement
    Sickness payments
    Holiday entitlement
    Hours of work and flexibility required.

15. Salary, commission, bonus etc.

16. Pension arrangements and terms.

17. Expenses and method of reimbursement.

18. Car or car allowance. If a car is to be provided, give details of make, model and cc as a guide. State the conditions and rules regarding private mileage. If an allowance is to be paid for the use of own car, give details.

19. Prospects offered by the firm:
    Financial
    Status.

Appendix B
Specimen
Personal Details Form

PERSONAL DETAILS OF:

SURNAME (FAMILY NAME) _____

FORENAMES _____

ADDRESS _____

_____

_____

_____

Telephone numbers _____ (home)

_____ (office)

Any restriction about calls?

Date of birth _____ Place _____

Married/single? _____ Children? _____

Education (give names of schools etc)

Primary _____

Secondary _____

Further _____

Examinations and principal subjects_____

_____

_____

Apprenticeships, articles etc _____

_____

(say where served and dates)

Membership of professional bodies with date of election_____

_____

Any serious illnesses since childhood?_____

_____

Any physical disabilities? _____

General health? _____

Are you prepared to undergo a medical examination?_____

DETAILS OF PRESENT OR MOST RECENT
APPOINTMENT

Employer _____

Address _____

_____

_____

Nature of business, product or service_____

_____

Turnover £ _____ No. employed _____

Date and title of first appointment_____

Commencing salary £ _____

Appointment now or last held_____

Responsible to _____

Date appointed _____

Number of employees for whom responsible_____

Present or last salary_____

Other emoluments _____

Please describe in detail the nature of your duties, the extent of
your authority and the responsibilities of the job.

_____

_____

_____

_____

_____

_____

(Continue on a separate sheet if you wish.)

Please give details of your earlier appointments on the form
overleaf.

ADDITIONAL INFORMATION.

Please give any further particulars which you think may be of interest, but which are not covered by this CV. Languages, knowledge of foreign countries, interests, offices held in clubs, societies etc.

Previous appointments

From/to (dates)	Company and address	Nature of business product or service	Position held	Duties	Final salary	Reason for leaving

Appendix C
Interview Record
and
Assessment

Date of interview _____

NAME _____

Appearance/manner _____

_____

Height _____

Build _____ Accent _____

Dress _____ Other features _____

_____

Family background _____

Work history _____

_____

Relevant experience _____

_____

Qualifications _____

_____

General notes and comments with reference to the job
specification

_____

_____

_____

_____

_____

Appendix D
Useful Literature and Sources

Department of Employment

(All booklets are available from Jobcentres, Employment Offices and Benefit Offices)

1. Written Statement of Main Terms and Conditions of Employment
2. Procedure for Handling Redundancies
3. Employee's Rights on Insolvency of Employer
4. Employment Rights for the Expectant Mother
5. Suspension on Medical Grounds under Health and Safety Regulations
6. Facing Redundancy? – Time Off for Job Hunting or to Arrange Training
7. Union Membership Rights and the Closed Shop Including the Labour Only Provisions of the Employment Act 1982
8. Itemised Pay Statement
9. Guarantee Payments
10. Employment Rights on the Transfer of an Undertaking
11. Rules Governing Continuous Employment and Week's Pay
12. Time Off for Public Duties
13. Unfairly Dismissed?
14. Rights on Termination of Employment
15. Union Secret Ballots
16. Redundancy Payments

Also:
Fair and Unfair Dismissal: A guide for employers

Individual Rights of Employees: A guide for employers
The Law on Unfair Dismissal: A guide for small firms
Industrial Tribunal Procedure
Code of Practice: Closed shop agreements and arrangements
Code of Practice: Picketing
A Guide to the Trade Union Act 1984

Advisory Conciliation and Arbitration Service (ACAS)

Advisory booklets (obtainable from any ACAS Office):

1. Job Evaluation
2. Introduction to Payment Systems
3. Personnel Records
4. Labour Turnover
5. Absence
6. Recruitment and Selection
7. Induction of New Employees
8. Work Place Communication
9. The Company Handbook
10. Employment Policies

Also:
The ACAS Role in Conciliation, Arbitration Mediation in Complaints by Individuals to Industrial Tribunals
Employing People – A handbook for small firms

Discussion papers
1. Developments in Harmonisation
2. Collective Bargaining in Britain – Its extent and level

HMSO

Codes of Practice
No. 1.   Disciplinary Practice and Procedures on Employment
No. 2.   Disclosure of Information to Trade Unions for Collective Bargaining Purposes

No. 3.   Time Off for Trade Union Duties and Activities

Work Research Unit, ACAS

St Vincent House, 30 Orange Street, London WC2H 9HH; 01–839 9281
Meeting the Challenge of Change: Guidelines for the Successful Implementation of Changes in Organisation (PL687).
Summary of publications: a listing of WRU published papers and other literature, regularly updated.
Organisation and Attitudes in Japanese Factories: a UK study tour of Japan (1983).

Further Reading from Kogan Page

Don't Do. Delegate! James N Jenks and John M Kelly, 1986
Effective Interviewing, John Fletcher, 1988
Effective Performance Appraisals, Robert B Maddux, 1988
Employment Law for the Small Business, Anne Knell, 1989
Executive Survival: A Guide to Your Legal Rights, Martin Edwards, 1988
Getting the Best Out of People, David Robinson, 1988
How to Solve Your People Problems, Jane Allan, 1989
Law for the Small Business, 6th edition, Patricia Clayton, 1988
Not Bosses But Leaders, John Adair, 1988
Readymade Interview Questions, Malcolm Peel, 1988
Team Building, Robert B Maddux, 1988

Appendix E
Sources of Information About Training

As stated in Chapter 13, every trade association and employers' organisation should be able to put its members in touch with an appropriate training body. Some, indeed, have close links with training boards or voluntary bodies who can offer guidance on particular aspects of any training requirement. Most professional institutes (eg accountants, marketing) also run courses from time to time.

The following bodies will also be helpful:

The Association of British Correspondence Colleges
6 Francis Grove, London SW19 4DT

British Association for Commercial and Industrial Training (BACIE)
16 Park Crescent, London W1N 4AP; 01–636 5351
BACIE will provide an up-to-date list of addresses and telephone numbers of organisations offering training.

Careers and Occupation Information Centre,
Moorfoot, Sheffield S1 4PQ; 0742 753275
Publishers of *Second Chances* – an annual guide to adult education and training opportunities (£9.95).

The Council for the Accreditation of Correspondence Colleges (CACC)
27 Marylebone Road, London NW1 5JS; 01–935 5391

Directory of Management Training
Bridgemore Park Enterprises Ltd, 71a High Street, Maidenhead, Berkshire SL6 1JX; 0628 75771

Educational Counselling and Credit Transfer Information Service (ECCTIS)
The *Directory of Educational Guidance for Adults* is free from ECCTIS, PO Box 88, Walton Hall, Milton Keynes MK7 6DB; 0908 368921
This includes lists of all local authority education and training advice centres.

Henley Management Centre
The Management College, Greenlands, Henley-on-Thames, Oxon RG9 3AU; 0491 517454

Institute of Marketing
Moor Hall, Cookham, Maidenhead, Berkshire S16 9QH; 0628 24927
The institute will provide details of courses in sales and marketing.

National Institute of Adult Continuing Education
19b de Montfort Street, Leicester LE1 7GE; 0533 551451
This organisation publishes a list of residential short courses every January and August.

PICKUP Programme
Department of Education and Science,
Elizabeth House, York Street, London SE1 7PH; 01–928 9222, ext 3564
PICKUP holds over 6000 records of short vocational courses for adults in a wide variety of subjects. The directory is available on microfiche, printed and floppy disk. (PICKUP = Professional, industrial and commercial updating.)

The Open University
12 Cofferidge Close, Stony Stratford, Milton Keynes MK11 1BY; 0908 566744
The Open University has 13 regional centres, to be found in most telephone directories.

Publications which give details of the main business studies courses:

Business Studies – free from Department of Education and Science, Elizabeth House, York Road, London SE1 7PH

BGA Guide to Business Schools – British Graduates Association, Canberra House, 315 Regent Street, London W1R 8DE; 01–637 7611

The above list should be adequate for all practical purposes in helping to find the right form of training in any situation.

Appendix F
Some Definitions and Other Useful Points

Dismissal

A person is treated as having been dismissed if:

- the contract is terminated without notice
- a fixed term contract is not renewed
- the employee terminates the contract and is entitled to do so because of 'constructive dismissal'.

Constructive dismissal

If an employer breaks some part of a contract of employment which is regarded as essential, the employee is entitled to leave and claim unfair dismissal.

Essential parts of a contract can be regarded as:

- a reduction in pay
- suspension
- reduction in status – possibly in relation to another employee.

Unfair dismissal

Dismissal is unfair, *ipso facto*, if it is because an employee:

- becomes a member of a trade union
- takes part, or proposes to take part, in trade union activity
- is in a group selected to be redundant, but was selected in contravention of an agreed redundancy selection procedure.

Misconduct

Gross misconduct can result in instant dismissal. It can be in the form of violence, drunkenness or total refusal to cooperate with company rules such as those on health and safety.

Otherwise, misconduct can be in the form of poor attendance, negligence or, perhaps, some outside activity which has a detrimental effect on the firm. To merit dismissal on this ground, there should be the process of warnings recommended in Chapter 15.

Redundancy

Redundancy occurs when a job ceases to exist because of changes in techniques, closures, cutbacks and so on.

Maternity leave

If an employer refuses to allow a woman to return to work after her confinement, she is regarded as having been dismissed on the day she notified her intention to return. She is unfairly dismissed unless she is made redundant and another job is offered.

Guidelines usually adopted by tribunals

Was there a fair reason for dismissal? Here the tribunal may not be as strict as a court of law. The employer has, nevertheless, to show he had reasonable grounds for taking drastic action. Even though company rules say instant dismissal will occur, employees should rarely be dismissed for a first offence. A crime is not always a good reason either.

Was a full and detailed enquiry made into all the circumstances of a case? Only that which was known at the time of dismissal is allowable. Knowledge which comes later is irrelevant.

Interim relief

Any employee can claim interim reinstatement while awaiting a hearing.

Index